OVERCOMING
THE POWER OF THE OCCULT

by

Terry Ann Modica

D1595703

First Published by: Faith Publishing Company

Published by: Queenship Publishing
                         PO Box 220
                         Goleta, CA 93116
                         (800) 647-9882 / (805) 692-0043
                         Fax: (805) 967-5843

Copyright © 1996, Terry A. Modica

ISBN: 1-57918-233-X
Library of Congress Catalog Card No.: 2003090527

Printed in United States of America

DEDICATION

To my husband, Ralph,
whose encouragement and support helped me write this
book;
to my children, David and Tammy,
who continually teach me about God's love and power,
and to our friend Father Ed Nichols,
who was the first to help me overcome
the power of the occult.

TABLE OF CONTENTS

FOREWORD

by Father Edward P. Nichols
September, 1996

A few years ago, I lived in a war zone. I was chaplain for approximately 1,500 U.S. Air Force men and women at a South Korean Air Base. The shooting war between North and South Korea had ended long before, but a peace treaty had never been signed. The two sides had only agreed to stop making direct attacks.

A state of war still existed, because the North Koreans were continuing efforts to infiltrate and covertly attack South Korea. At the base where I served as chaplain, the Koreans had live ammunition at the machine gun posts and anti-aircraft positions. They had tanks at the gates. Every month, the U.S. troops and the South Koreans held joint exercises, wearing combat gear and carrying chemical warfare suits. We were practicing how to respond if and when we came under attack.

In a very similar way, we Christians live in a war zone. This book clearly describes the tactics and weapons that Satan and his demons use to stealthily attack us — from Ouija boards to psychic powers to the deceptive teachings of the New Age movement.

Whether we like it or not, Satan and his aides and followers are like the North Koreans. They are trying to sneak in and confuse us to lead us away from God and His power. We must acknowledge that we are in the middle of spiritual warfare and use the power of God to overcome the power of the occult. We *must* pay attention to *Ephesians* 6:10-13 (NIV):

*Finally, be strong in the Lord and in his mighty power.
Put on the full armor of God so that you can take your
stand against the devil's schemes. For our struggle is
not against flesh and blood, but against the rulers,
against the authorities, against the powers of this dark
world and against the spiritual forces of evil in the
heavenly realms. Therefore put on the full armor of God,
so that when the day of evil comes, you may be able to
stand your ground, and after you have done everything,
to stand.*

I know from personal experience how real and sneaky
and powerful Satan is. In my twenty-one years as a priest,
I've often seen the need for spiritual warfare. I've prayed
with many people who couldn't understand why their
physical or emotional problems were not healed by simple
prayer. They needed to renounce various evil spirits that
were blocking them from receiving God's power of healing.

When those with this need seek appropriate guidance
and support, then renounce the demons and receive prayers asking Jesus to send the demons away, a change
occurs. The bondage of unloving attitudes is broken and
God's unconditional love flows in. I've seen it happen
dramatically.

This book outlines the reality of the occult's power,
and it teaches how to overcome it with the greater love
and power of God. Everything written here is in complete
agreement with the teachings of the Roman Catholic
Church. Especially helpful are the appendices on prayers
for help, danger signs of the presence of evil powers, the
deceptions of the New Age movement, and the two-
hundred-plus Scripture quotes about the occult and God's
greater power.

We live in a war zone amidst the strongest and most
devious enemy ever created. I wish this book didn't have

to be written. But it did. I wish you didn't have to read it. But you do, so that you can use the power and love of God to win the most deadly war ever raged.

PREFACE

When I was seventeen years old, I announced that someday I'd write a book showing that reincarnation and other parts of the occult complement rather than contradict Christianity. More than two decades later, my dream came true—with a major difference. The purpose of the book changed. I've learned fascinating insights about reincarnation and other occult subjects that I couldn't understand back then.

I've learned that, compared to all the supernatural power offered by the occult, the very best comes from God Almighty. His power is loving. Real. Permanent. Glorious. His power provides answers. His power is far more exciting and dependable than anything I had imagined.

Although I was raised in Christianity, something had been missing: the supernatural power of God. I began to actively seek it at age fourteen by exploring the occult. After seven years of searching, I finally found it, but only after looking beyond the occult.

For another twelve years, I studied, tested, learned, studied, tested and learned. Finally, a supernatural event inspired me to sit down and put it all into a book from which others can study, test, and learn.

It happened at the St. David's Christian Writers Conference in Pennsylvania. I was trying to put my occult experiences into an article, but I kept failing to come up with a workable ending. I thought, "Maybe this should be a book." But the publishers at the conference were not interested in my idea, especially since I had no written proposal, no outline, and no sample chapters to prove I could do the work.

At the end of the week, I stood in the dinner line next to the one publisher I had never considered. In the course of non-related chit-chat, he asked me what writing project I was working on. I told him my occult book idea. His eyes widened and he replied, "I'm looking for just such a book!"

I knew then that our meeting had been no accident: God had arranged it.

Never mind that a writer normally has to send his or her book to dozens of publishers before it finds a home — *if* it gets published at all. In a supernatural way, I knew that I had found my publisher and that God was telling me to go ahead and write about overcoming the power of the occult. The finished product reached the bookstore shelves in 1990.

Six years later, when I least expected it, God did it to me again. All the copies of my book had been sold and the publisher was not going to reprint it because they had gone out of business. But Bill Reck of Faith Publishing tracked me down (not an easy task, since I had moved from New Jersey to Florida) and told me he wanted to reprint it. My conclusion: God's not done using this book; it's time to revise it and make it available to those He chooses.

You who are now reading these words, be assured of this: It was no accident, no happenstance that put this book into your hands. Neither was it luck, nor human decision alone. God has chosen you. He wants to help you because He loves you and is bringing victory into your life.

I haven't written this book alone. From the beginning I've had plenty of supernatural help, including an angel sitting to my right. I've also had a wonderful husband, Ralph, encouraging me in this endeavor, even though it meant my income virtually stopped while I researched and wrote, even though sometimes he'd come home from work to find me still at the computer instead of at the stove cooking dinner.

Thanks are due to my mom and dad, Pam and Don Repsher, who taught me much about how to find the love of God. Extra hugs go to my children, David and Tammy, who continually show me the power of pure trust. And to the many, many people who have fought for this project through the prayers of spiritual warfare, may their generous help be multiplied right back to them.

I especially pray that God's blessings will cover each person who holds this book in their hands. May you find the true answers.

Terry Ann Modica
September 1996

Chapter 1

In Search of Supernatural Power

It started with a Ouija board. My search for supernatural power began at the same age when many people first become entranced by the occult—I was almost a teenager. I assumed the Ouija board was just a game. I believed what I'd heard: that it worked by releasing hidden answers from my subconscious mind.

But one Sunday afternoon, my younger sister, Karen, and I got an answer that surprised us. Neither of us could have pulled it out of our youthful minds.

"What is the meaning of church?" we had asked the Ouija.

We expected it to reply, "A place of worship," or perhaps, "God's house." Instead, the triangle-shaped pointer, with our fingers barely touching it, moved around the alphabet to spell P-E-O-P-L-E.

"You're making up a false answer!" Karen and I accused each other. To settle the matter, we asked our father if the meaning of church could be "people."

"Why do you ask?" he replied.

"The Ouija board said it was," we told him.

"Well, it's right," he said. Then he explained how the Church is not a building of wood and stone, but everyone who worships God.

Now, *this* was exciting. This seemingly simple game could provide an accurate answer beyond our knowledge! Karen and I wanted more supernatural answers. We never once stopped to wonder where the answers came from. Playing with the Ouija was fun; that's all that mattered to us. Therefore, when the next opportunity came to learn more about the occult, I eagerly took it.

1

On my fourteenth birthday, a friend gave me a book on haunted houses. This opened a whole new world of mysteries. Hungry for more, I frequented the bookstore and library to devour everything I could find on ghosts and spirit communication.

My favorite author was "ghost hunter" Hans Holzer. His books taught me about another plane of existence, an afterlife that I'd never heard about in my Christian upbringing. He described it as a place between Heaven and Earth through which everyone passes after death. Some, he said, get stuck there and become the ghosts who haunt houses. Holzer had even photographed and tape-recorded a number of these ghosts.

Two years later, I was to see and hear his proof of life-after-death at a lecture he gave at my high school. Meeting him helped to firm up my confidence in his ideas.

Meanwhile, I longed to experience the spiritual world myself. At the same time, my curiosity led me to books on related subjects. One of those was hypnotism.

An idea hit me: If I could hypnotize my sister, maybe I could put her into a mediumistic trance so she could channel a ghost. The opportunity came, one evening, when we were alone with a friend. We turned out the lights, lit a candle on the coffee table between us, and settled into our chairs.

At first we giggled, but then I began to lull the two of them into a hypnotic state using the words I'd memorized from a book. When they responded to a few suggestions, indicating they were deep in a trance, I told them to look with their inner eyes into the spiritual world.

"What do you see?" I asked.

"Someone's here," the friend mumbled.

"Who?" I leaned forward. "A spirit?"

She shook her head. "It's gone now."

After I brought Karen and our friend out of their trances, they both reported sensing a presence in the darkness they had entered.

"Could it have been a spirit?" I asked.

"Probably," they replied.

We were hooked. Eager to share our discovery and improve our skills, we invited other friends into our circle and formed a secret club, *The Psychic Society*. I taught a classmate to be hypnotist, and the two of us guided our friends into trances.

Usually we contacted "spirit guides." We believed them to be the souls of dead people who had the special assignment of helping us, sort of occult counterparts to guardian angels. They temporarily possessed our mediums' bodies to speak to us.

One of the things they told us was why they had taken an interest in us: because we were involved in the occult. They wanted to encourage us to pursue it further. That should have sounded an alarm in us, but we didn't want any doubts to stop us from having our fun.

In our seances, these "guides" took over quickly. We sought their help in locating everything from spirits we could talk with to lost pet hamsters. We never found the hamsters (we assumed the cat had reached them before we did), but we often met what we believed were troubled souls. Some, apparently, were ghosts who didn't know they had died; some sought our help in finding deceased loved ones; others were angry and needed to find peace.

This gave a purpose to our seances. We could help these spirits!

"Look for God," I'd tell them, and as soon as I began to talk about God's love, they'd leave. We thought we had steered them into Heaven.

Ghosts started seeking us out, sometimes making themselves known by creating cold spots near us in the house.

The more involved I became, the more I wanted to learn. Nothing was as fascinating as the occult. My curiosity spread to witchcraft, reincarnation, Tarot cards, astral projection, automatic writing, and almost anything I came across. The only occult field I never tried was Satanism, because I didn't believe the devil existed. This disbelief turned out to be one of the reasons I trusted the occult.

My life took a sudden, unwanted turn after I turned seventeen. My family moved from southern New Jersey to upstate New York. No one there wanted to join us in Psychic Society number two.

A new friend, Janet, gave me a book that explained why all spirits contacted in seances are really demons trying to fool us to convince us we don't need God. If this were true, it would explain why the ghosts always left when I started talking about God's love. But that's not what I thought had happened, so I disregarded the author's warning.

Little did I know I was soon to experience proof of this first-hand.

In my last year of high school, I met the young man who would later become my husband. I told him it would be fun to get hypnotized and visit the world beyond. Unwilling to say "no" to the girl he wanted to impress, he agreed.

"You are going deeper and deeper into the spirit world," I monotoned as he sat on my parents' couch, trusting me. "Look around you with your spiritual eyes."

Ralph's body began to quiver nervously and he awoke with a start. His eyes locked on me with intense fear.

"What happened?" I asked.

"I can't talk about it." He stood up to leave.

"Ralph, what did you see?"

He hesitated, shaking his head. "It wasn't anything like you said it would be."

"Did you see something?"

He shivered. "A huge, hideous figure. Dark and shadowy. Cold." He paused. "It reached out to get me." He turned to get out of my house as fast as his feet permitted. "It was evil. Very evil."

Despite his frightening experience, I still wanted to try again, although not with Ralph. The opportunity never came, but I continued reading more and more about psychic phenomena. In college, I even took a course on it.

When Ralph and I married, we moved to Florida. Our new lives did not include church because we couldn't find one that felt right to us. By this time, I couldn't be satisfied with a church that did not believe reincarnation is an alternative path to Heaven or that Christians are called to evangelize ghosts.

After so many years of making God part of my daily life, I wanted to live without Him. After so many years of seeking the supernatural, I turned my back on the greatest supernatural Being in the universe.

Would I have drifted away from God had I never gotten involved in the occult? It's impossible to know, but one thing is certain: The involvement ruined my relationship with Him. My Christian beliefs had been warped by the occult and left me with no awareness of a need for God or for the Church that the Ouija board had described as people.

I had fallen victim to the biggest danger of the occult. I **had used it to develop my spirituality.** I had thought it would lead me closer to God and Truth. In the end, it destroyed what I had sought to gain.

That's what happens when people get involved in the occult. As unlikely as it seems at first, it eventually ends in destruction.

It usually starts quite innocently, for the best of reasons. Dabbling seems safe. What harm could reading the daily horoscope do if you don't take it seriously? What's wrong with talking to a fortune teller if she says her ability is a gift from God? Why worry about playing with Tarot cards if you believe it's only a game?

Humans hate the unknown. We don't feel secure until we know the answers. If we experience something that intrigues us at the fun-and-games level, our curiosity makes us want to know more.

This process is quickened by a need to satisfy our spiritual cravings. Since we are not merely physical beings but also spiritual, we, in Western societies, search for greater fulfillment either through the religion in which we were brought up or through Eastern mysticism, Stephen King novels, Shirley MacLaine-type experiences, and anything outside the realm of rational, scientific teachings.

But this search can be dangerous, because the spiritual world consists not only of good, but also of evil. There are angels and there are demons. There is the Holy Spirit and there is the Evil One.

Even psychotherapists recognize a danger. According to occult expert Kurt Koch, they are finding an increasing number of neurosis cases "which in many observed instances stand in noteworthy frequency ratio to the increasing occult practices."[1]

Many people attribute all things spiritual either to God or to some impersonal, transcendent force. Then they can feel safe dabbling in whatever they want. But they are heading for destruction.

Such was the case of Paulette S. It started early in her childhood. She remembers trudging to Catholic school, wondering, "Why do I feel so empty? There's gotta be something more. What am I missing?"

The nuns taught her about the man on the crucifix that hung in every classroom, but that alone didn't seem to answer her questions.

"If there is a God," she wanted to know, "why did He put me here?"

These questions shadowed her into adulthood. Marriage didn't fill the void. Neither did giving birth to three boys, although these were, certainly, wonderful events. She began to wonder if fortune telling might provide some answers. Throughout her childhood she had heard her mother and her aunts talk about the psychic powers that ran through the family. Perhaps her purpose in life was to use psychic gifts to help others!

In her mailbox, she found an advertisement for an occult book club that claimed to hold the answers to the universe. Thinking that at last she'd found what she was searching for, Paulette joined and ordered books on nearly every topic. She learned to improve a precognitive (knowing future events) talent that seemed to come naturally for her, and she began to tell fortunes with cards.

She devoured everything written by Jeane Dixon and Ruth Montgomery, reasoning, "Since these psychics are powerful, they must be getting all kinds of answers!"

Astrology provided some answers, so she absorbed enough of it to recite anyone's characteristics based on birthdates.

She found reincarnation especially intriguing. She attended hypnosis classes to uncover her past lives, although she never discovered any. She thought the knowledge would come as she developed more skill.

She joined a local psychic group and learned psychometry (reading an object to learn things about its owner). A typical success was the time she concentrated on a man's wedding ring and saw a plane land at an airport.

"Amazing!" the man said. "My wife just came back from California!"

Still, with all she learned, a few questions remained unanswered. "Why am I here?" As talented as she had become, none of her gifts really helped anybody.

Then her life fell apart. After more than a decade of marriage, she found herself in the midst of a stressful divorce. The aching void inside her grew.

Looking back at that time, she realized that the occult had left her unprepared for marital problems. "The things I was becoming talented at," she said, "Satan was giving to me. But he lies. Further down the line, when you're getting good confidence in your talents, all of a sudden the rug comes out from underneath, because he's got you."

Paulette had ended up with a ruined relationship and no solutions. She felt more miserable and hopeless than she ever had before she'd gotten involved in the occult.

What Is the Occult?

Everyone seeks answers. We all need something supernatural to lift us out of difficult problems and give us meaning for our lives. But where do we turn for the best answers, the strongest power, the greatest fulfillment?

The occult *seems* to offer what we want. The word "occult" comes from the Latin word *"occultus"*: hidden, secret, mysterious. According to *Webster's Third New International Dictionary*, "occult" as a noun means "the action or influence of supernatural agencies." As a verb, it means to deliberately hide from sight, "to conceal or extinguish the light of by intervention."

The word "light" is a key to understanding the occult. The supernatural agencies behind the occult conceal and extinguish light. What is meant by this? What kind of light?

"Light" is often used as a symbol of truth. In Judeo-Christian terms, it represents the ultimate truth, i.e., God, the Messiah, Christ. Jesus called Himself "the Light of the world." Therefore, it can be said that the supernatural agencies behind the occult deliberately intervene in our lives to conceal or extinguish the Light of Christ or the Light of Truth. This certainly proved true in my own life when it destroyed my relationship with God.

The purpose of this book is to show just how this concealing of the Light occurs and what we can do to overcome the darkness. In so doing, I share the sentiments of an early Christian, St. John Chrysostom, who said to the people of Antioch, "It certainly gives us no pleasure to speak to you of the devil, but the teaching which this subject gives me the opportunity to expound is of the greatest use to you."

Why Is the Occult Growing in Popularity?

The power of the occult entices increasing numbers of people today, because it deals with secret knowledge and hidden power. It fascinates us with events or abilities that go beyond the normal. It conjures up spiritual forces that make an inviting alternative to the physical and materialistic problems so rampant in our world.

The occult offers much: 1) knowledge, 2) excitement, 3) prestige, 4) a sense of belonging, 5) a connection to the universe, 6) quick results, 7) power beyond our human limitations, and, of course, 8) immortality.

1) **Knowledge**: We're born curious. Knowledge is a coveted prize, especially secret knowledge. People involved in the occult tell us: Maybe you haven't found the answers you seek because they lie hidden. If you contact a higher intelligence from the unseen spiritual realm, you will finally uncover them.

2) **Excitement**: Experimenting with occult powers is exciting because they're exotic and forbidden. The scientific world tells us that the occult is nonsense. Others say it's evil. But much of it looks both genuine and good. So why not play with the forbidden fruit? If we don't eat the whole apple, what harm can there be?

3) **Prestige**: You can be the center of attention at parties if you know how to read palms. If you can discuss astrology intelligently, your friends will start coming to you for advice. And imagine how impressed everyone would be if you discovered you were a Mayan king in your past life!

4) *A sense of belonging*: Human beings are social creatures. We need to be accepted by others. We can find approval for our interest in the occult if we join a psychic study group. We can eliminate the aloneness we feel if we

belong to a cult or a coven where everyone shares our beliefs.

5) *A connection to the universe*: As astronomers discover more and more about the infinitely vast universe, we feel increasingly insignificant: "Who am I, this infinitesimally tiny creature on a small, overpopulated planet lost in one arm of one galaxy among many? What part do I play in the large scheme of things?" If we study astrology or think we are contacting extraterrestrials we can believe we are one with the universe. We are not, as we fear, unimportant.

6) **Quick results**: The occult is appealing because it seems to be an easy way to get what we want. Cast a spell and make your wish come true. Throw some cards on the table and figure out the future now. Draw up an astrological chart and discover immediately if the guy (or girl) you're dating is right for you to marry.

This is fast-food spirituality. "Western men want results, they want action, they want bright lights and communion with God. Furthermore, they want these things in no more than three easy lessons,"[2] said Dr. Gary North, president of the *Institute for Christian Economics* and author of numerous books. Sometimes God doesn't answer our prayers fast enough for our liking, so the occult seems more powerful.

That's why a seventy-year-old widow, who'd been a church-going Christian for forty years, turned to the occult. When her non-Christian husband died, she longed to know if he'd gone to Heaven. She begged God to reveal her husband in a dream. But the dream never came. Her desire for an answer increased until, finally, a spiritualist told her she could have her wish. "You can see your husband again," said the spiritualist, "in a seance."

The widow jumped at the chance. During a very pious-looking ceremony, the wall of the room became brightly lit. What seemed to be her husband appeared in the light-field. His face looked horrible and he rode a billy-goat toward her.

Fear gripped the woman. After that, deep depression set in, along with thoughts of suicide. It became impossible to pray or read scripture. None of these problems had ever happened to her before. They came as a direct result of seeking answers through the occult.

7) **Power beyond our human limitations:** The occult is powerful, certainly. It makes things happen that have no scientific or human explanation. Some people actually foretell events. Others levitate. Some mentally control the movements of objects or people. Some cast spells that work too often to be called coincidence. But this power never fully satisfies. More often than not, it leads to bigger problems than those it was supposed to solve, as happened to Paulette.

8) **Immortality:** "There is an irrepressible longing to live forever," wrote Pope John Paul II in his apostolic letter *Towards the Third Millennium.* "How are we to imagine a life beyond death? Some have considered various forms of reincarnation." Why bother with Christ's salvation if reincarnation is available to all? Spirits tell us in seance after seance that the human soul is immortal, unkillable, and they seem to give proof of a reasonably happy immortal existence.

The occult entices many, at least sixty-five million in the United States, and many more millions in Europe and around the world. Those who fall prey to the occult include: the curious who don't know with what they're really playing; the conformist who gets involved because others do; the bereaving who want to end the pain of separation; the gullible who are too easily convinced of supernatural events while giving little thought to the dangers; the troubled who've found little help from conventional sources; the rebellious who get involved because it's forbidden; people who seem to have psychic talents and want to believe their gifts are good; and children who are exposed to it in the family.

Almost all who are not born into it start out in search of truth; but those of us who try the occult are lulled into thinking we have found ultimate reality. We are influenced into believing we no longer need to search for truth.

This actually goes against our inborn desire to persevere until we find the truth that totally satisfies our craving for love. Pope John Paul II addresses this in his encyclical letter *The Splendor of Truth*. He says that our curiosity cannot ignore the obligation to ask the highest and purist of all questions. He adds:

> Rather, it spurs us on to face the most painful and decisive of struggles, those of the heart and of the moral conscience. No one can escape from the fundamental questions: What must I do? How do I distinguish good from evil? The answer is only possible thanks to the splendor of the truth which shines forth deep within the human spirit, as the Psalmist bears witness: "There are many who say: 'O that we might see some good! Let the light of your face shine on us, O Lord,'" (*Psalm* 4:6).

The light of God's face shines in all its beauty on the countenance of Jesus Christ, "the image of the invisible God" (*Col.* 1:15). . . . Consequently the decisive answer to every one of man's questions. . . is given by Jesus Christ, or rather is Jesus Christ himself.

In searching, whether we realize it or not, we are actually seeking a Messiah — someone or something that can save us from our problems. There's much in life we can't handle alone, but people are undependable or unconcerned. Stable families are rare. The future seems uncertain, *if* it exists. Our air may be poisoned. The economy falters while the national debt grows. The rate of crimes, suicides and mental illnesses is ever rising, while morality is sinking. Wars overlap wars — everything's in danger and it's all out of our control!

"This world is in need of a shining light and longs for the supernatural flame of charity" (i.e., the love that is Jesus Christ), said Pope Paul VI in an apostolic letter released on August 6, 1966.

Sadly, fewer and fewer people are interested in turning to the Christian Church to find this "supernatural flame." Back in 1957, eighty-one percent of Americans believed religion could answer the world's problems, according to the *Princeton Religion Research Center*. By 1989, that figure had dropped to sixty-one percent.

Over the years, religion has lost its importance. Before the occult became popular, seventy-five percent of Americans thought religion was **very** important (according to 1952 Gallup poll).

Then the decline began. By 1978, only fifty-two percent believed religion was very important. Since then, it's not improved much. In 1994, fifty-eight percent considered religion very important. And yet, for many of these people, it's **not** important to participate actively in their religion. Church attendance is way down: The same Gallup survey revealed that a mere thirty-two percent attend church or synagogue at least once a week, and another fourteen percent attend almost every week, bringing the total of church-goers to forty-six percent. According to a 1988 Gallup poll, only ten percent can be considered "highly committed spiritually."

In other words, many people like to consider themselves religious, but few have any real commitment to God. Few truly understand that He loves us no matter what, and offers us very real, very powerful, supernatural help through His Son Jesus. With Christianity seeming so apparently empty and powerless, it's no wonder that people turn to New Age religions.

The situation is even worse in European countries. A *World Values Survey* conducted in 1990-1993 found that in western Germany, only eighteen percent attend at least one worship service per week; in Britain, fourteen percent;

in France ten percent, and in Sweden, a mere four percent.

The faith journey of "baby boomers" (a large population group of people born between 1945 and 1954) reflects what's been happening in America. Wade Clark Roof, Ph.D., a sociologist of religion at the University of California Santa Barbara, found that two-thirds of the baby boomers dropped out of church in their teens for two or more years. Of these drop-outs, twenty-five percent rediscovered the importance of Christianity when they began having families of their own. As a result, according to a study by David Roozen, professor of religion at Hartford Seminary in Connecticut, church attendance (of all age groups) climbed from thirty-three percent in 1975 to forty-one percent in 1990.

However, nearly twice as many of the drop-outs (forty-two percent) have stayed away.

Many of them are now in mid-life, when they are most vulnerable to being proselytized by New Age ideas. Mid-life is a time of seeking what's been missing. They're rearranging their priorities. They're looking for something meaningful to which to commit themselves. And their quest for spirituality and self-fulfillment has become too strong to easily ignore.

Most of those who believe in angels are baby boomers and those under thirty. "It is evidence, in part, of the spiritual hunger in this country," said George Gallup Jr. of the Gallup polling organization. "There is a deep searching going on. People want to grow in faith; they want spiritual moorings in their life."

Most (ninety-five percent) believe in God, including those who refuse to recognize that New Age spirituality can lead them away from God. Four out of five believe in life after death; the same number believe in miracles. But the question is: What kind of life after death do they believe in? What (or Who) is the source of the miracles?

Look at how many people own a Bible and compare that to how many actually use it to bring them into the greatest possible spiritual growth. According to the *American Bible Society*, nine out of ten own a bible, but only twenty-seven percent use it. Many cannot even recite the names of the four gospels.

When God's love is not shared powerfully enough with those who are searching, they fail to realize that He has the supernatural answers and power they seek. The occult seems to be the only alternative.

Psychotherapist and author Dr. Rollo May has said, "The lapse into the occult is a way of managing anxiety."

Episcopal Bishop Paul Moore, Jr., once said, "People have to believe in something. So they turn to anything that comes up . . . religion on the cheap."

Today's "religion on the cheap" has become known as the *New Age Movement*. The term "New Age" refers to the modern explosion of occult practices and the blending of Eastern mysticism with Western pop psychology.

The movement has its own powerful evangelization efforts, through television shows and movies, advertisements for psychic helpers and witchcraft lessons, occult supplies offered in catalogs and New Age shops, public libraries and bookstores with entire sections devoted to the occult, and psychic fairs in shopping malls.

There are New Age restaurants, churches, travel companies, doctors and health centers, even New Age health care facilities for dogs and cats. There are New Age grocery stores, drug stores, counsellors, public relations firms, and money managers. It has its own music, magazines and tours to sacred sites. It has conventions in which are sold music and videos, clothing and furniture, juice and mushrooms, lotions and crystals, massage therapy and psychic readings. And there are radio shows with phone-in channeling (consulting with spirits).

Channelers are getting rich. Week-end seminars cost from $150 to $600 (in some cases, $1500) per person, with six hundred to eight hundred people willing to pay this *per session.* Private consultations generally cost up to $250 per hour. By the time people become disillusioned and quit consulting channelers, they've spent thousands and thousands of dollars!

Publishers are also profiting greatly from the New Age movement. Bantam Books increased their New Age line ten times in the 1980s; it's been their fastest-growing nonfiction product. Ruth Norman, who self-published over ninety books, video and audio tapes on reincarnation, channeling and the like, started a newsletter that has 600,000 subscribers. Shirley MacLaine's book *Out on a Limb* sold four million copies **before** the movie was televised in 1987.

By 1987, there were 2,500 New Age bookshops in the United States, a number that doubled in five years. Regular bookstores have large New Age sections.

Psychic Guide, a magazine that features "interviews" with dead celebrities (John Lennon reported there's sex in the afterlife!), had 125,000 subscribers in 1989. *New Age Magazine* had 130,000 paying readers. Because angels have become a popular New Age topic, *Angel Times* magazine was first published in 1994; its circulation quadrupled to 100,000 in one year.

The students who've attended *Free Soul,* a psychic training program in Arizona, number over 25,000. An amazing sixty percent of them are professionals and business people.

According to Andrew Greeley's National Opinion Research Center, in 1986, one-third of the population believed they had some degree of clairvoyance. Around the same time, the University of Chicago's National Opinion Research Council found that forty-two percent believed they'd contacted the dead, and sixty-seven percent claimed to have had psychic experiences. A 1983 Gallup poll reported that one in four Americans believes in reincarnation. A 1990 Gallup survey found that forty-six percent believe in psychic power, thirty-six percent in telepathy and twenty-four percent in astrology.

In 1989, the Princeton Religion Research Center reported that fifty-eight percent of teenagers believe in astrology, fifty percent in E.S.P., twenty-nine percent in witchcraft, and twenty-two percent in ghosts.

Whether or not all of those percentages can actually be confirmed, it is still obvious that New Age evangelization is winning over increasing numbers of people to a growing number of alternative spiritualities. Around 1960, there were less than 100 religions in the United States, including cults. The non-Christian religions have increased so prolifically, there are now close to one thousand religions. One mystical religion, called the *Unity School of Christianity* (which is **not** Christian: it teaches that we are all Christs and that Jesus is not the Savior), saw a thirty-four percent increase in five years. By the end of the 1980s, three million people were reading their publications.

New Age evangelization is even infiltrating Christian churches, sneaking in through yoga (which traditionally is a quest for mystical union with the Hindu spiritual god-force), some forms of guided imagery, mind control classes, stress management based on Eastern mysticism, meditation that doesn't focus on Jesus Christ, seminars on astrology, and the like. Even the YMCA (lest we forget, "C" stands for Christian) sponsors psychic fairs and Tarot classes.

Robert Burrows, a researcher for the *Spiritual Counterfeits Project*, a non-profit organization in Berkeley, California, that studies trends in cults and the occult, said of occult activities infiltrating the Church: "They seem to point to a Church that has lost touch with its rich spiritual heritage, and in its hunger for a deeper spiritual life, absorbs indiscriminately whatever is in the cultural wind."[3]

For example, a former Roman Catholic priest, Matthew Fox, of Oakland, California was reprimanded by the Vatican in 1988 and sent on a year's sabbatical for incorporating New Age philosophies into his teachings. Fox had founded the *Institute of Culture and Creation Spirituality* and had become popular on the New Age lecture circuit. His faculty included a masseuse, a yoga instructor, a Zen Buddhist and a witch. Courses included Body Prayer, Dances of Universal Peace, Tai Chi, and Cosmos as Primary Revelation. Not exactly Christian theology.

The fact that some New Age philosophies are good (in a strictly psychological sense) along with the fact that many of them incorporate Christian language, confuses many truth-seekers. Proponents even insist that New Age concepts are compatible with Christianity. Gina Clare, director of a New Age community in New Jersey, said: "We celebrate all religions, all spiritual paths that care for the common good." Doesn't that sound commendable? She makes Christians feel guilty for believing that Christ is the only true Savior.

The confusion is compounded by vague titles such as Fox's "Cosmos as Primary Revelation." (A revelation of what?) The problem is not new. In the early days of Christianity, St. Paul warned us in 2 *Timothy* 3:7-9 (NJB) about people who follow one craze after another:

> *Always seeking learning, but unable ever to come to knowledge of the truth . . . these men defy the truth, their minds corrupt and their faith spurious. But they will not be able to go on much longer: their folly . . . must become obvious to everybody.*

In the search for supernatural power, there is one source that's often overlooked. It is stronger. It is more fulfilling. It is more exciting. It is more dependable than anything the occult offers.

The greatest power comes from the Creator of the universe. God has supernatural love for each of us, and to enable us to receive His love and to help others with it, He gives us His supernatural gifts. He heals incurable diseases, restores failing marriages, overcomes impossible circumstances: He gives us whatever is most loving.

Let's look again at what the occult offers and compare it now to what God offers.

1) **Knowledge**: The occult tell us: Maybe you haven't found the answers you seek because they lie hidden. But God says, "I love you. I will never hide from you the answers you need. I will reveal whatever is good for you when I know you can best handle it. All that you seek can be found by sharing your life with Mine, reading and learning from My Word, and trusting Me to take care of you. You can believe everything I tell you, because I never lie to you or mislead you. If there's something you don't understand, ask Me, and I will help you understand. You might have to wait, but I will always answer in the most loving way. It might not be the answer you want, but it is always what's best for you."

2) **Excitement**: There is nothing more exciting than allying with the Creator of the Universe. When we choose to follow His lead, journeying under His guidance, and ridding ourselves of the desires to go in other directions, we can do the same works that Jesus did and even greater works (see *John* 14:12). We become His partners making a significant difference in the world.

3) **Prestige**: Why bother becoming the center of attention through reading palms or giving astrological advice when you are a child of the King of all creation? His kingship makes you a royal prince or princess. If you choose to work with Him, you become an ambassador for His kingdom. Think about how special you are based on the fact that you even exist. When your parents conceived you, there were 200 million different possibilities for life. God chose you out of all those options. That makes you very important.

4) **A sense of belonging**: No Christian is truly alone. If we belong to Christ, we are part of the same family; we

belong to each other. If you attend a church that seems large and cold and you feel like nobody cares about you, join one of the smaller groups that your church offers, such as the choir, a prayer group, a Bible study, or a club that helps the needy. When you make the effort to find other Christians, you find support and encouragement. God delivers His love to us through each other.

5) **A connection to the universe:** You are God's child; you are a masterpiece He's created (God never makes junk). You are unique and can never be replaced. There is no reason to feel insignificant. He will help you discover why He created you. It will take time to prepare for, develop and enter into His special purpose for you, but each day has its own opportunities for God to utilize your particular talents, skills and experiences.

6) **Quick results:** We're used to microwaving quick meals and pushing a few buttons to instantly talk to someone on the other side of the country, so we want God to work just as fast. However, He usually seems to work way too slowly to suit us. Even though His timing is always perfect, we don't believe it because we don't like waiting. But the moment we turn to Him for help with anything at all, He responds. He embraces us with His love and His assurance, He sets the wheels of change in motion, and He provides us with everything we need to survive the wait. To experience this quick help, we only have to be alert and pay attention.

7) **Power beyond our human limitations:** God, too, makes things happen that have no scientific or human explanation. He works miracles through us when we've made ourselves available by growing in an ever-deeper relationship with Him, following His ways. This is the power that fully satisfies. You'll learn more about it in Chapter 12.

8) **Immortality:** In the kingdom of God called Heaven, we will live in complete joy and peace and love forever, and we only have to die once to achieve it. While we are

on Earth, if we've chosen to do things God's way, we are already living in His kingdom. Therefore, the joy and peace and total love of God comes to us here and now. This is possible because Jesus (Who is the only one both fully human *and* fully God) died for us on the cross, taking our sins with Him, and then God our Father raised Him from the dead. Thus, through Jesus we have a glorious immortality guaranteed.

But seventy-eight million American adults do not know this.[4]

The reason so many people don't know that God offers something better than the occult is because Christians have been too quiet—even ignorant—about God's love and power. Yet Christians have in their hands (or musty closets) what could be called the Book of Loving Power and All Truth—the Bible. We live in a biblically illiterate society.

Too often, "the Christian faith gets watered down to a pale reflection of the culture and values of society," said a United Methodist minister, Rev. Guy Whit Hutchison, in 1989, while chaplain for the American University in Washington, D.C. "We need to make clear what faith really is, recover the excitement."

Roman Catholic Cardinal James A. Hickey referred to this problem at the *Fellowship of Catholic Scholars* in 1989. He said that contemporary Americans have lost a sense of the sacred, but millions are fascinated by the terrifying, the occult and the vaguely supernatural.

The New Age movement is "an endless quest for novelty and stimulus in every direction and the satisfaction of appetite," wrote Jesuit priest Daniel Berrigan, in a 1987 article for *Omni* magazine. Harper and Row's Clayton Carlson has said that New Age books sell extremely well because people are "questioning the meaning of it all. They're finding that the traditional systems aren't working, and are taking alternative per-spectives more seriously."

Hutchison noted that, among young adults, "there's a sense of powerlessness. There's an inner need to turn to some other place where they can feel powerful and excited."

Franciscan Father Benedict Groeschel has also observed this problem. As director of spiritual development for the New York Archdiocese, he told parochial teachers at the 1988 High School Institute in New Jersey, "There are tremendous numbers of young people in the United States . . . who are desperate. They look for salvation, redemption and meaning in life. They have left the Church and religion and they don't know where to go. Some of the young people in your classrooms are involved in the occult."

Father Mike Carroll, a high school teacher from Wisconsin, has said that the popularity of the New Age movement seems "to point out the failure of our traditional institutions to respond to a desire to believe."

This is backed up in a survey by the *National Conference of Catholic Bishops*. It found that young people show "a new openness to and interest in religion," but often turn away from the Church because they find it "impersonal" and "inhospitable." No wonder one in ten Americans who were raised Catholic no longer identifies with the Church, while fundamentalist churches are growing in membership. The solution, the report says, is programs that are "effective in assisting young people to *experience* Christ" (italics mine).

God has what everybody seeks. To help people discover the power of God, there's much that Christian churches can do. They can make faith an experience rather than an intellectual exercise. They can make the supernatural gifts of God tangible and teach how to receive them. They can show why Christianity offers more power than Eastern mysticism and the occult. The key to accomplishing this is to make God's love real to the seekers by loving them the same way Christ loves us — unconditionally reaching out and serving them.

But over half of all adults (fifty-nine percent) say churches aren't doing this. They are complaining, according to a 1988 Gallup poll, that most congregations are "too concerned with organizational as opposed to the theological or spiritual issues."

A 1989 study of growing churches in New Jersey revealed that those with the largest increases in membership were family-oriented, back-to-the-Bible churches with activities designed to reach all age groups.

Paul McGuire, author and Hollywood filmmaker, has warned of the fierce fight the New Age movement is waging. He said, "Universally, people have a God-given desire to discover God. But Christianity has not presented itself to our culture on a mass level, especially to our young people. There-fore people turn to the occult and Eastern mysticism. The root of the problem is that Christians don't take Christianity's role seriously."

He added that the reason Christianity seems impotent is because throughout Christian culture there is "the false view of spirituality which says being in church is spiritual, while working for the *New York Times*, for example, is not spiritual." To make biblical Christianity more real, he said, "I believe in miracles. Yet this talk about miracles is always off someplace in Oklahoma or Texas." In other words, Christians must bring the power of God right to where people live. God's love isn't just for sharing in church; it must go out to all of the people around us.

Every Christian has "countless opportunities for exercising the apostolate of evangelization and sanctification," agreed all the Roman Catholic bishops of the world during Vatican Council II, writing in the *Decree on the Apostolate of Lay People*. "We are apostles commissioned by God to love the way Jesus loved by living the way Jesus lived. The very witness of a Christian life, and good works done in a supernatural spirit [i.e., unconditional love through which we readily forgive and serve others], are effective in drawing all to the faith and to God."

Many who become involved in the occult skirt the edges of Christianity and miss the answers they seek. Instead, they see a Church that seems powerless to halt the flood of increasing immorality. They see a Jesus who offers lots of *dos* and *don'ts* but not much love and victory. They see pastors who preach a watered-down Gospel. They see Christians who are more a part of this world and its problems than they are overcomers and ambassadors for the Kingdom of God. They see Christians who fail to condemn the occult because they either don't believe in it or they're afraid of it. And they see an oversystematic, abstract, intellectual religion that dwells in the head, not in the heart, where love is a nice word but is not lived out in daily encounters with others.

Therefore they do not see a God who can meet their needs right now, right here, with power. God warned about the results of this. To those in positions to teach about God, He said (*Hosea* 4:6 RSV):

> *My people are destroyed for lack of knowledge;*
> *because you have rejected knowledge, I reject*
> *you from being a priest to me.*

Paulette, who'd been so close to the knowledge of God in Catholic school, was nearly destroyed by her lack of knowledge. After her divorce, she remarried, but the void from unanswered questions still raged within her. She tried to drown it out by watching TV shows that might provide answers. She came across *The 700 Club*. This Protestant talk show revealed something she hadn't discovered before: a God who both cared about her problems and had the power to do something about them.

Paulette phoned one of their counselors for help. The woman at the other end prayed with her, then suggested that Paulette look for an *Aglow Women's Club* in her area.

Within a week, Paulette found one. At the meeting, the speaker asked everyone who wanted to know the Lord to stand up and be prayed for. Paulette decided to give Christ a chance to answer her questions and fill her void.

From that moment, her life changed. She discovered a far greater supernatural power than anything she'd experienced in the occult. Here was a supernatural source that cared about her! Jesus Christ gave her power to get through the rough times without the usual anxiety. And she felt His assurance that the future, with Him in it, would be good. He gave meaning to her life. The old emptiness was finally gone. Completely! The something more she had always sensed missing was the inner presence of God's Divine Son.

What a difference from her occult days. She had never found any of her psychic powers to be truly satisfying. "It was always just a little bit to keep me interested, keep me searching," she said. "But as a Christian, I've laid hands on people and prayed over them, and I've seen healings. There's nothing I can't do with the help of the Lord!"

---

[1] Kurt Koch, *Christian Counseling and Occultism*, Grand Rapids, MI: Kregel Publications, 1965.

[2] Gary North, *Unholy Spirits*, Fort Worth, TX: Dominion Press, 1988, p. 357.

[3] Robert J.L. Burrows, "Americans Get Religion in the Age," *Christianity Today*, May 16, 1986, p. 23.

[4] According to a May, 1988 Gallup poll, 78 million people are unchurched, i.e., have not taken part in religious worship in the past six months other than for special holidays, weddings, or funerals.

Chapter 2

Deceptions

There's a whole world of supernatural power outside of God's realm. How can we know what is and what isn't from Him? How can we know what leads to truth and what leads to danger?

Carol of Cimarron, Kansas, was raised in a mainline Protestant church, but at an early age she realized that what was preached on Sunday was not necessarily what people did the rest of the week. Even though she gave her life to Jesus, she found that something in her faith life was lacking.

In her search for truth about life, death and the hereafter, she turned to astrology, levitation and other forms of the supernatural. She read many books on the occult and a few on Satanism. Up till then, she hadn't believed that Satan really existed, but his power was becoming more obvious in her life. Things kept going wrong.

She realized her life was never going to be the way she wanted it, despite the help offered by the occult, so she dulled her frustrations with alcohol. Eventually, the drinking became uncontrollable. She told me, "When the time finally came when I could no longer drink and couldn't quit, I fell to my knees and gave myself to Jesus once more." She asked Him to take over her problems and to fill her life with His presence.

In return, He revealed His true power. He gave her a miracle. And He sent it through a messenger, an angel.

"On that night," she said, "an angel came to me, offered me his hand and gave me back my life. My obsession to drink was instantly lifted and I have not had the desire to drink in the three years since."

She added, "The truth I'd looked for all my life, of course, was God's Son, Jesus."

Many people believe that the occult offers truth. But we have to wonder: If it can't save them from problems such as divorce and alcoholism, what good is such "truth"? If it can't save them from eternal separation from God, what good is it?

The only real Truth is the kind that helps us with problems, frees us from anxiety and fear and inner turmoil, and saves us from eternal aloneness (which is one description of Hell). Anything else is deception.

The occult offers spiritual experience, but what does it lead to? When Jesus walked the earth, He fed people who were spiritually hungry, but He didn't just lead them into a spiritual experience. He led them into a deep relationship with His Father, our Creator.

Therein lies the key to true supernatural power and eternal happiness. Without a deep relationship with our Creator, we miss the best supernatural power of all and we miss the eternal joy of living with Him in Heaven.

Eastern meditation — from Zen to transcendental meditation to yoga — has deceptively woven its way into Christian prayer. Because this is a growing problem, the Vatican, *Congregation for the Doctrine of the Faith*, put together a document approved by Pope John Paul II in 1989. Titled *Some Aspects of Christian Meditation*, it warns that attempts to fuse Christian meditation with non-Christian methods are "not free from dangers and errors."

The danger, it says, is that these methods either ignore or abandon the saving works of God. They also reject the idea of the one and triune God, who is Love. Does this mean that all forms of non-Christian meditation should be avoided? No, as long as we use them to focus on the sacrificial love of Christ and the gift of His Holy Spirit.

The occult is not a neutral force. There are supernatural forces behind each of its practices. Using them costs us something. We cannot get in and out of the occult freely.

In his book *Kingdom of Darkness*, F.W. Thomas cited an example of its lasting effects. In London, a husband-and-wife journalist team decided to investigate the occult. They joined a satanic group to gain first-hand knowledge, then quit because of the horrible rituals they witnessed. They were never the same again. They endured terrible experiences and incidents. Their lives became filled with anguish and despair.

Thomas wrote, "One cannot just pick up the dark bolts of magical fire and drop them at will without getting burned. There is always a price to pay for use of these forbidden powers, in this world as well as in the next."[1]

"At the heart of all magic is the quest for power, but at low cost," Gary North has said. "Economically, it is the philosophy of something for nothing." The problem is, he pointed out, "the price of their power is far, far higher than they think."[2]

If we believe it's safe to seek supernatural power without going to God for it, we are deceived.

As St. Thomas Aquinas wrote in his *Commentary on John*, "It is better to limp along the true way than to walk fearlessly apart from it. A man may limp along the true way and seem to advance but little, yet he does draw near to the goal; but all the tireless running on the wrong road only takes one farther from the goal."

The New Age movement leads us away from God's supernatural power. Look at the central message of the New Age. It says we don't need God. It says we can rely on all sorts of substitutes. It says we don't need to seek a closer relationship with God because we are God.

As author Paul McGuire has said of the New Age, "It has a naive attitude toward evil." He pointed out that all New Age things become idols. "New Age methods become substitute saviors, false messiahs, false gods. That's why they're dangerous."

It means the New Age movement offers spiritual

shortcuts. It says we can have happiness, fulfillment and spiritual enlightenment without submitting ourselves to God, without getting rid of the evil in our lives.

How can we be certain we've found real truth if we don't submit ourselves to God? How can we be sure we're not experiencing counterfeits from evil forces? How do we know we're not falling short of the tremendous gifts we could have? (For a comparison of God's gifts and the New Age movement, see Appendix C.)

We can't be certain of any truths unless we first check them out with God, through a relationship with His mediator, Jesus Christ. There are **many** ways into the spiritual world, but there is only **one** way to the Father, and that is through His Son, who said in *John* 14:6 (TLB):

> *I am the Way — yes, and the Truth and the Life.*
> *No one can get to the Father except by means of*
> *me.*

One of the common deceptions we hear today is that there is no God, at least none who cares much about us. This lie is popular because it allows us to feel safe while using supernatural powers that don't come from God. We ourselves might even be spreading this lie because God hasn't answered our prayers the way we want Him to.

What is the original source of this lie? Who would want to promulgate this lie? Satan, of course.

However, many people choose to believe that Satan and other demons don't exist. If they don't believe in demons, they can feel safe living without God. There are even Christians who refuse to believe. For example, a survey of Catholic college students on the East Coast revealed that more than three fourths reject the idea of a devil. And yet, more than eighty percent said they either believe in angels or had been in contact with them. A 1994 Gallup poll found that seventy-two percent of the general population believes in angels. That's a significant increase from 1978, when only fifty-six percent did. Angels are very popular in New Age ideologies because people want supernatural beings to be real without demons being real.

This is dangerous, because believing in the reality of demons is necessary so they can be properly and effectively dealt with. It is so necessary that in the Roman Catholic Church, the organization responsible for clearly and accurately communicating the teachings of the Church Magisterium — the *Sacred Congregation for the Doctrine of the Faith* — has issued a paper on this subject, entitled *Christian Faith and Demonology*. The first concern they address is people's disbelief in demons, noting that "the idea of Satan. . . has lost its importance."

Previously, Pope Paul VI had said, "It is a departure from the picture provided by biblical and Church teaching to refuse to acknowledge the Devil's existence; to regard him as a self-sustaining principle who, unlike other creatures, does not owe his origin to God; or to explain the Devil as a pseudo-reality, a conceptual and fanciful personification of the unknown causes of our misfortunes."

To say that Satan and his demons are mere myths is to say that Jesus was subject to delusions and inconsistencies, because He dealt with them and spoke about them as if they were real. Either that or we deny He was divine with knowledge beyond the ideas of the times.

Consider what Jesus believed about Satan and other demons. During the forty days He spent in the desert before His public ministry, He defeated Satan using His knowledge of Scriptures and trust in God the Father. Later, He healed people by specifically commanding demons to depart from them. If the devil were simply a myth, then why did exorcisms work, and why do they still work? Why did Jesus warn His disciples about the "power of hell" (*Matt.* 16:18) or that Satan would sift them like wheat (*John* 14:30)? Why did He spend time during the Sermon on the Mount teaching people to guard against Satan and to end the "Our Father" prayer with "deliver us from the evil one" (*Matt.* 6:13)?

According to Protestant theologian John Newport, "Jesus could not have deliberately taught a false theory of demons." He clearly saw his ministry as a conquering of Satan. Belief in Satan points "to the seriousness of man's need and (is) a reminder of the absolute necessity of God's grace."[3]

Satan was also very real to the early Church. Paul wrote in *Ephesians* 6:12 (NJB):

> *For it is not against human enemies that we have to struggle, but against the principalities and the ruling forces who are masters of the darkness of this world, the spirits of evil in the heavens.*

As mentioned in *Christian Faith and Demonology*, Paul "exhorts us to resist Satan (*Eph.* 6:11-16), never to give him a foothold (*Eph.* 4:27, 1 Cor. 7:5) and to crush him beneath our feet (*Rom.* 16:20). He also described Satan when he said in 2 *Corinthians* 4:3, 4 (NJB):

> *If our gospel seems to be veiled at all, it is so to those who are on the way to destruction, the unbelievers whose minds have been blinded by the god of this world, so that they cannot see shining the light of the gospel of the glory of Christ, who is the image of God.*

Notice what Paul said about Satan blinding people from seeing the light of the glory of Christ. Satan tries to occult Christ. This is Satan's primary goal, which he often achieves through deception. Jesus said in *John* 8:44 (NJB):

> *He was a murderer from the start; he was never grounded in the truth; there is no truth in him at all. When he lies he is speaking true to his nature, because he is a liar, and the father of lies.*

Therefore, Satan can never be trusted. Carefully, cunningly, he makes the occult seem good and full of answers, even though it's dangerous and full of lies. That's why Dr. F. LaGard Smith, professor of law at Pepperdine University and expert on New Age deceptions, has said, "Today, the need for discretion is urgent. Virtually always, there is a residue of truth involved in the deception—just enough to entice us. Just the right amount to confuse us."

How can we know what is truth and what is deception? How can we know what is from God and what is from demons?

Dr. Smith answered that: "In order to exercise discretion properly, we must familiarize ourselves with God's word. In the New Age with which we are confronted, having only a superficial understanding of broad Christian themes will leave us vulnerable to spiritual counterfeits." The Bible—God's Word—contains all the answers we need.

The Apostle Paul, who experienced first-hand the supernatural power of God, said in 2 *Timothy* 3:16 (NJB):

> *All scripture is inspired by God and useful for refuting error, for guiding people's lives and teaching them to be upright.*

And Jesus said in *John* 8:31, 32 (NJB):

> *If you make my word your home . . .you will come to know the truth, and the truth will set you free.*

Since God is all goodness and incapable of lying, the Bible teaches us the ultimate truth. To correctly understand the Bible and avoid misinterpretations, we should not just be our own teachers. We need first of all the Holy Spirit to guide us. Then we need to go to resources provided by experts who have remained faithful to the knowledge that's been passed down from the beginning of Christianity.

The Roman Catholic Church has many such resources. It has published short books (called "documents" or "encyclicals") on innumerable topics, all of which are based on Scripture, explain Scripture and relate Scripture to practical everyday uses. Before they're published, these documents are carefully scrutinized to make sure the teachings are in line with the truths that Christ passed on to His apostles.

With solid grounding in correct understanding of the Bible, we can compare what it says to New Age teachings; we can find out what is truth and what is deception.

The Bible teaches us how to identify New Age deceptions:

> *If anybody does not remain in the teaching of Christ but goes beyond it, he does not have God with him* (2 John 9 NJB).

> *Beware of false prophets . . . You will be able to tell them by their fruits . . . a sound tree produces good fruit but a rotten tree bad fruit* (Matt. 7:15-17 NJB).

> *The fruit of the Spirit is love, joy, peace, patience, kindness, goodness, trustfulness, gentleness and self-control* (Gal. 5:22, 23 NJB).

Look at the lives of New Age people. What are their fruits? Are they self-indulged or truly loving? What is most important to them: their own happiness? Money? Power? Success? Or God, Who can provide all we need. Do they have an inner peace beyond understanding, the way Christ can give it, or does fear rule their lives? Are they using their gifts to make a significant improvement in the world, as happens when we work for God?

Jesus offers all the answers we seek, all the love, joy and peace we need — which is precisely what Satan doesn't want us to find out.

The Roots of Deception

Today's New Age is not new. Its roots go back to a very ancient movement known as Gnosticism. It's challenged Christianity several times, especially during the first three centuries after Christ and during the Middle Ages. It bypasses the doctrine of the Trinity: God as Father, Son, and Holy Spirit. We have inner power, it teaches, that comes from an impersonal divine and cosmic force. In the 1880s, this evolved into a religion called Theosophy. Invented by a Russian spiritualist medium, Madame Helena Blavatsky, it was a blend of half-understood versions of Buddhism and Hinduism. Madame Blavatsky mixed this concoction with stories of Atlantis, ancient Egypt and other "lost civilizations."

Theosophy failed to influence Western culture until the 1960s when dissatisfaction with the "establishment" grew strong. Stirred up by spiritual hunger and fascination with the supernatural, other aspects of the occult and mystical religions were added in, creating the New Age movement we have today.

There is as yet no indication that the growth of this movement will slow down. Authors John Naisbitt and Patricia Aburdene noted in their book *Megatrends 2000* that the New Age movement, as one form of spirituality, will play an ever-expanding role in our world.

New Age followers are hoping that the movement will expand enough to encompass all religions and spiritualities, eliminating, of course, those aspects they don't like, such as the need for Christ as Savior. An example of how they've done this is the religion of Mannu, founded by astrology guru Linda Goodman. To create Mannu, she took the teachings of St. Francis of Assisi that dealt with our relationship to "brother" sun, "sister" moon and other creations of God, discarded his strong devotion to Jesus Christ, and added in the mystical beliefs of Native American Indians. Many Christians, especially Catholics, assume that because St. Francis is part of it, Mannu must be good and of God.

New Agers would like to see the world governed under a single headship. Supposedly, this would bring an end to wars, unevenly distributed wealth, etc. The Bible warns that before the second coming of Jesus an Anti-Christ will appear who will rule the world. A New Age world ruler who tries to supplant the need for Jesus might indeed become the future Anti-Christ. Individually—now —we need Christ to come to us a second time, in the fullness of His glory, to bring us into full conversion to God's love.

The New Age uses three main themes to pull people away from God: belief in 1) the decline of civilization, 2) a coming New Age and 3) knowledge gained from other civilizations.

1) *Belief in the decline of civilization* describes a gloomy future, the imminent destruction of society. They include the prophecies of Nostradamus. We even find this theme in some of the alleged apparitions of the Virgin Mary.

2) *Belief in a coming New Age* offers hope and optimism for a self-destructing world. The dawning of the Age of Aquarius, an astrological idea, is supposed to save the world through humanism, brotherhood and the occult.

3) *Belief in knowledge gained from other civilizations* holds that the world's salvation from destruction will come, thanks to the scientific superiority of lost or extraterrestrial civilizations. This is why a 1987 Gallup poll found that most Americans believe UFOs are real. A 1991 Roper survey revealed that 3.7 million people in the U.S. think they've been abducted by space aliens. To find out how impossible this is, multiply 3.7 million by 22 to extrapolate worldwide. If each "abductee" is visited five to ten times in a lifetime, as many claim, then extraterrestrials have dropped by half-a-billion times, amounting to 5,000 per hour every day!

Superior civilization beliefs include myths of a past

golden age before recorded history, from which mankind has fallen—a counterfeit of the Judeo-Christian concept of the Garden of Eden. This mythical fall supposedly result-ed in a loss of mystical powers; salvation would then come from regaining those powers through the occult.

All of this, of course, is deception. These beliefs are nothing new. Doom-sayers have been around for centur-ies. Historically, their pessimism has been revived every fifty years or so, but most especially at the turn of each century, and even more so at the turn of a millennium, as we are now experiencing. Such need for rescuing by extraterrestrials denies the hope that Jesus Christ offers. It assumes that God is not powerful or caring enough to give us a good future.

New Age beliefs take our focus off of Jesus Christ, the true Savior of the world. Humankind's fall from perfection came because of sin—the very same sin the New Age movement promotes, i.e., trying to become God rather than submitting to God. It will not be the advanced tech-nology of an extraterrestrial race that saves our world, but the second coming of Christ, at which time all evil will be destroyed. We need not even wait for this, for Jesus can and desires to overcome the evil we're each experiencing right now. We have only to ask and trust Him.

New Age deceptions are everywhere. I found in my mailbox one day a newsletter from a New Age "ministry." It mentions God frequently, but it perverts God's Truth.

The issue I received claims Jesus prayed this before the first Easter: "Father, glorify me with your own self, with the glory which I had with you before the world was."

It needs to be read *in context* (*John* 17:1, 2 NJB) to understand Jesus' intent:

> *Father, the hour has come: glorify your Son so*
> *that your Son may glorify you; so that, just as*
> *you have given him power over all humanity, he*

*may give eternal life to all those you have
entrusted to him . . . Now, Father, glorify me
with that glory I had with you before ever the
world existed.*

The New Age says: "Glorify me." Jesus says: "Glorify
me by raising me from the dead so that I may glorify you,
Father, by giving eternal life to those who believe."

New Age proponents who use the name of Jesus and
misquote Scriptures to trick people (intentionally or not)
are blaspheming God. They might not realize it, but they
are Satan's tools. Their words and actions may seem
respectable, but behind the deception is immense, satanic
power. St. Peter warned in 1 *Peter* 5:8 (NJB):

*Keep sober and alert, because your enemy the
devil is on the prowl like a roaring lion, looking
for someone to devour.*

Let's look at why Satan wants to devour us.

Ezekiel, while equating the prince of Tyre (one of
Israel's enemies) with Satan, described the devil's fall from
Heaven: He had once been a model of perfection, full of
wisdom, perfect in beauty; his behavior was exemplary
until guilt first appeared in him; he became filled with
violence and sin; his heart grew proud because of his
beauty (see *Ezek.* 28:12-17).

God created Satan as the highest and most beautiful of
angels, but Satan was not satisfied. He wanted to be greater than God. So he rebelled. This is described in *Isaiah*
14:12, 13 (NJB):

*How did you come to fall from the heavens,
Daystar, son of Dawn? How did you come to be
thrown to the ground, conqueror of nations?
You who used to think to yourself: I shall scale
the heavens; higher than the stars of God I shall
set my throne.*

During the fifth century A.D., Pope St. Leo the Great noted that "God, the Creator of the universe, made only what was good. This is why the devil himself would be good if he had remained in the state in which he was created. Unfortunately, since he abused his natural excellence and did not remain in the truth (*John* 8:44). . . he separated himself from the supreme good." In 1215, the *Fourth Lateran Council* of the Roman Catholic Church officially clarified this doctrine and stated that "the devil and the other demons were created naturally good by God, but it is they who by their own action made themselves evil."

Satan had been one of the three greatest angels with Michael and Gabriel, but he led some of the lower angels into rebellion. *Revelation* 12:7-9 (NJB) says that as a result:

> *War broke out in heaven, when Michael with his angels attacked the dragon. The dragon fought back with his angels, but they were defeated and driven out of heaven. The great dragon, the primeval serpent, known as the devil or Satan, who had led all the world astray, was hurled down to the earth and his angels were hurled down with him.*

Paul told us in 2 *Corinthians* 11:14, 15 (NJB) how Satan continues to lead the world astray:

> *Satan disguises himself as an angel of light. It is nothing extraordinary, then, when his servants disguise themselves as the servants of uprightness.*

Ruth Norman, the founder of a popular occult organization, has called Satan "a true bearer of the light." Here's her history of the devil, according to the organization's literature: ". . . Satan (who was a very real human being with an exaggerated ego) and his many helpers, taught his people erroneous and detrimental concepts while on planet Tyron. . . . But now—and this is the infinite truth—he, too has changed!"

Lies from the father of lies! Only Jesus Christ—who is God Himself—is the true bearer of light. He said in *John* 8:12 (NJB):

> *I am the light of the world; anyone who follows me will not be walking in the dark but will have the light of life.*

This is the only path to reaching our full potential in the realm of the supernatural. No wonder Pope John Paul II begins *The Splendor of Truth* with these words: "Called to salvation through faith in Jesus Christ, 'the true light that enlightens everyone' (*John* 1:9), people become 'light in the Lord' and 'children of light' (*Eph.* 5:8), and are made holy by 'obedience to the truth' (1 *Peter* 1:22)."

Anyone who denies that Jesus offers the best enlightenment and the greatest potential is either deceived or a liar. Proof of this is found in 1 *John* 2:22 (NJB): *"Who is the liar, if not one who claims that Jesus is not the Christ? This is the Antichrist."*

Those who blaspheme Jesus (such as satanists), deny Him (paganists) or subvert His message (as cultists do) are acting the part of an anti-christ. Members of these groups may be sincere, but sincerity is no protection from the delusions of Satan.

Satan counterfeits all gifts and truths of God to make himself look as much like God as possible (2 *Thess.* 2:9). His purpose is to trick us into following him into eternal punishment. "By deceiving man he leads him to projects of sin and death, making them appear as goals and fruits of life," says Pope John Paul II in his encyclical letter *The Gospel of Life*. Whether it leads us to occultic activities or the deaths of unborn children through abortion, the devil gives us many "good" reasons to reject God's gifts and the real truths.

He even makes God appear to be our enemy, as John

Paul II points out in *The Holy Spirit in the Life of the Church and the World:*

> The spirit of darkness is capable of showing God as an enemy of his own creature. . . . as a source of danger and threat to man. In this way Satan manages to sow in man's soul the seed of opposition to [God] . . . . Man is challenged to become the adversary of God! . . . There will be a constant pressure on man to reject God, even to the point of hating him: "Love of self to the point of contempt for God," as St. Augustine puts it. Man will be inclined to see in God primarily a limitation of himself, and not the source of his own freedom and the fullness of good.

The devil is extremely jealous of anyone who is headed for Heaven. He knows that the only way he can hurt God is by snatching His children. It's no surprise, then, that Satan's sin is also the sin of the New Age movement: believing that we are equal to or better than God. It's been Satan's theme from the beginning. When he tempted Eve in the Garden, he promised that if she ate the forbidden fruit, she could be like God (*Gen.* 3:5).

The forbidden fruit of the New Age (see Appendix D for scriptures on what is forbidden) keeps us from going to God and His supernatural love. Dianne Core, founder of *Childwatch* (for the protection of children), has said, "The New Age is a glittering and shimmering path into the abyss that blinds people so that they no longer recognize their Creator."

She said that, since its beginning, "the priests of the New Age understood their craft. They knew how to seize on people at their weakest and most vulnerable spots, and give them an apparently correct answer to their problems."

It's easy to succumb to the temptations of the New Age, especially if we fail to recognize Satan's activity. We laugh at the image of a little devil on our shoulders whispering into our ears, but Satan does try to plant his thoughts into our minds. Such "planted" thoughts do not mean we're demon-possessed, just that demons are actively fighting against us and against God. We need to learn to recognize their ideas and reject them.

True wisdom lies in humbly admitting that some of our beliefs might be wrong and then asking the Holy Spirit to reveal the truth.

Dr. F. LaGard Smith has described what can happen if we fail to ask the Holy Spirit to teach us the truth about the occult: "If Satan can tempt us with seemingly innocent practices, he thinks he may just get that foothold he is looking for." Smith adds that simply taking our minds off of Jesus Christ and the power that we can have through Him allows Satan to accomplish his mission—often through practices that even appear to be Christian. We need to listen to the Holy Spirit. We need discernment.

How discerning are we? We watch—and allow our children to watch—entertainment that contains some of Satan's propaganda. We glance at the newspaper's horoscope or psychic predictions. Public schools (and even some Christian schools) stock up on books about the supernatural (although books on God or Christian beliefs are taboo). Schools even invite guest speakers on witchcraft, astrology, fortune telling and mind power.

Horror movies are horrible, since they encourage a fascination with evil. They glamorize the vileness of the kingdom of Satan and draw many, especially teenagers and young adults, into the search for supernatural power through occult means. Many have such a high degree of occult realism they become training films.

Soap operas (both daytime and prime-time varieties) don't often deal with the occult, but they are Satan's tools nonetheless. Filled with cheating, lying, fornication, lust, nastiness, revenge, and myriad other sins, these shows never project God as someone to turn to for help. The Bible warns us to avoid these shows: "Keep away from people like that" (2 *Tim.* 3:2-5). They set bad examples and desensitize us to immoral conduct and attitudes.

Rarely is God depicted in the media as a loving Father eager to share His supernatural help (with the amazing exception of a few miraculous shows, such as *Touched by an Angel* and its kin). Indeed, we rarely hear God's name at all on television or in the movies. When the good guys win, it's usually through their own deeds. On the other hand, the bad guys often exhibit satanic symbols, even in cartoons. The message is: Its okay to talk about the devil but not God, because we don't need God.

How effective is Satan's propaganda through the media? Can his demons actually reach us through the screen?

Linda* was a Christian teenager who had never been involved in the occult. Her mother, Arlene*, had made its dangers clear. But when advertisements for a movie about witchcraft piqued her curiosity, she went to watch it at a friend's house. Some scenes included spells and chanting, but as long as she didn't imitate the characters, what harm could it do?

When she returned home, she found three of her siblings and a couple of their friends in the living room talking to Mom about the love and power of Christ. Linda glared at her mother and said, "You stop this now."

Surprised at her daughter's manner, Arlene said, "What do you mean? We're having a discussion about —."

"You heard me. Stop it." She enunciated each word slowly. Turning to the kids, she said, "You get out of here!"

Arlene stood up. This was not like her daughter. Something wasn't right, and it was frightening the kids.

Since Linda was trying to break up a discussion about Christ, Arlene deduced that a demonic force was behind her daughter's unusual behavior. So she said, "Linda, in the name of Jesus Christ, you leave now!"

The girl glowered, turned and fled from the room.

Arlene told the others, "I'll find out what's going on. But first, let's get rid of this fear that's here now." Remembering what the Bible says about spiritual warfare, she commanded, "In the name of Jesus Christ, you spirit of fear, I bind you and send you away from this house." Then she said more gently, "Children, you say the Lord's Prayer while I'm gone."

Arlene went to the stairs, whispered a prayer for God's help, and went to Linda's bedroom. She found her daughter lying face down across her bed.

"What's wrong?" Arlene asked.

Quiet sobbing was the response.

An idea stirred in Arlene. "Did you go to somebody's house and get involved in something?"

Linda propped herself on one elbow. She looked frightened. "I didn't listen to you, Mom. I watched that movie."

By exposing herself to the occult, Linda had unwittingly picked up a demonic presence. As a Christian, she could not be possessed by it, but she had brought it home. It was that spirit who had been so disturbed by the discussion downstairs.

Arlene commanded the spirit to leave by binding it and casting it away (explained in Chapter 10) from her home in the name of Jesus Christ and told Linda to say the name of Jesus.

The moment Linda uttered the name, she began to cry and buried her head in her mother's shoulder.

At the very same time, they heard a loud "Praise God!" from downstairs. When Arlene went to investigate, the kids were jumping with excitement.

"Something happened!" they shouted. "It felt like the

roof of the house lifted up and a bright light came into the room!"

The children had been unable to hear anything said in Linda's bedroom, but they knew, somehow, a breakthrough had occurred.

My own breakthrough came after seven years of occult involvement. My curiosity had pulled me so far away from God, I no longer saw a need to turn to Him for anything. But this was not the kind of life God wanted for me. He wanted me to experience more love. He wanted me to utilize greater gifts and power than what I had settled for. And He wanted to protect me from the disasters I was surely headed for (the disasters of earthly ilk and of eternal separation from Him).

So He inspired a Jesus-filled Catholic priest to phone me. Father Ed Nichols and I had been pen pals for years, but we had lost touch. As we chatted, he unexpectedly asked if he could come to visit Ralph and me for a week of his vacation time. Not long after, as he sat in our living room sharing his love with us, I noticed the difference between his life and mine. He never said a word of condemnation about my interest in the occult or the fact that I no longer went to church. He simply revealed Jesus by the way he cared.

·I felt a longing stir up within me for the power of God's presence. I thought I could get it without giving up my interest in the occult, so I turned my life back over to Jesus Christ and asked the Holy Spirit of God to fill me.

I discovered He offers something more exciting than occult powers. He gave me the answers I needed. My inner emptiness disappeared. I discovered that, through Him, miracles are possible—miracles that work out better than anything we could ask for or imagine.

Since the Holy Spirit is the Spirit of Truth, He shed His light on all my occult beliefs. One by one, as I held them up to the Scriptures, He showed me that He condemns every aspect of the occult. And He showed me that He offers far better alternatives.

Looking back, I could see how Satan had used my naive interest in the occult. Using my curiosity, he had drawn me deeper and deeper into the occult, thus pulling me farther and farther from God and His truth.

That's why the Ouija board had worked so well. That's why my awkward attempts at seances had worked. That's why "spirits" sought us out to communicate with us.

I had thought everything was due to my own "superior" abilities and God's help. I didn't want to believe in demons. I didn't want to see the truth, because then I would've been faced with the decision that you, too, face:

God or the occult?

---

* Not their real names

---

[1] Cited by Clifford Wilson and John Weldon, *Occult Shock and Psychic Forces*, San Diego, CA: Master Books, 1980, pp. 13, 14.
[2] Gary North, *Unholy Spirits*, Fort Worth, TX: Dominion Press, 1988, p. 271.
[3] Dr. John Newport, *The Biblical and Occult Worlds: A Twentieth Century Confrontation* tape series, Fort Worth, TX: Latimer House Publishing Company, 1973, "The Christian, Demons and Exorcism."

Chapter 3

The Ouija Board: First Step on a Dark Road

By age twenty-two, Joanne's* fast, efficient secretarial skills had already earned her the well-paid job of executive secretary. Beautiful, intelligent, always smartly dressed and eager to do her best, she was admired by friends and co-workers.

The first to notice a change in her were her friends at church. Although she had dated one of the members of the Catholic Youth Organization only briefly, she began to monopolize his time. The group thought this odd.

Once when Mike arrived home from work, he found Joanne parked in his driveway. After chatting a few minutes, he excused himself, saying, "You've got to go, now. I have to get supper ready for my dad and me."

A few days later she followed him home from the grocery store. This time she stayed in his driveway waiting for him to come back out of his house.

As this behavior continued, Mike confided in his friends.

"It's really beginning to get to me," he told them. "How can I get her to leave me alone?"

"Call the police," Joe* suggested.

"How could I do that? I don't want to hurt her."

"I'll talk to her," Connie* said.

Connie found her opportunity the next day at the snack shop.

"I'm in love with him," Joanne crooned. "He's being a little stand-offish, but I know he loves me."

"Are you sure?" Connie said. "He told us you're bothering him."

"Oh, yes. He loves me." Connie could not convince her

otherwise.

That night, around 6:00, Mike called Connie on the phone. "Get Joe and come over here. Joanne's here and I can't get her out of the house." Connie heard scuffling. The phone went dead.

She called Joe and the two hurried to Mike's house, eight minutes away. When they knocked on the door, no one answered. They went around to the back. No answer.

Not knowing what else to do, they returned home and hoped Mike would call again. The phone finally rang at two in the morning.

"Connie, she's in the back yard near the trees. I've gone out and talked to her, but she's like an animal."

"What happened? We went over and no one answered the door."

"I had to get out of the house because she was trying to get in."

"Call the police."

"No, no. My father wouldn't be able to take it."

"Well, I can't come over at this hour, so lock up the house and go to bed."

The next day, Mike went to work not knowing if Joanne was still in the woods. When he came home, he found her sitting in his living room.

"How'd you get in?" he asked.

"I walked through the door."

"The door was locked."

"Your father opened it."

"My father's an invalid. He can't get out of bed."

She shrugged and smiled. Mike tried to convince her to leave, but the look of cold terror in her eyes frightened him. He went to the phone to call Connie. Joanne ran out the door.

When Connie and her friends arrived, Mike said, "Maybe you ought to go find her. She's in a real bad way, emotionally. Who knows what could happen."

They searched the neighborhood, the bars and park.

After a couple of fruitless hours, Connie went to Joanne's home.

"She's out with her boyfriend, Mike," Joanne's mother said.

Connie told her what had really happened. "Do you know what's going on with her?"

"I've seen nothing unusual," the mother said. "She goes to work every day, seems fine to me."

Later that night, Mike called Connie again telling her Joanne was in his bedroom, and had broken into the house.

Mike agreed the problem was out of control, but as he dialed the police, Joanne darted through the hall and fled out the door. No one could find her for two days. She didn't go home. She didn't go to work.

On the night of the second day, Mike came home and found her in the kitchen. She looked like she'd spent all that time in the woods.

"How'd you get in?" he demanded.

She shrugged and flitted around the room. "You left a basement window open."

"Does my father know you're here?"

"I told him you asked me to take care of him. You need me."

"Joanne. Please leave us alone. I don't want you to come back any more. If you try this again, I'm going to have to get a restraining order put on you."

"How can you say that, darling?" she pouted. "I love you. You're the man I'm going to marry. I know you love me, too."

Mike took a step backward. "I've never done anything to make you believe that."

"You love me, Michael."

"No, I don't. I never have!"

Joanne screamed. She jumped on Mike, arms swinging, hitting him in the face and on the chest. Mike grabbed her arms. They were cold, ice cold. They were stronger than he was. He maneuvered behind her and picked her up bodily, pushed her to the door, then shoved her out. He slammed it shut and leaned against it. Joanne started beating on the door, shouting that she loved him.

Mike called the police, but by the time they arrived Joanne had disappeared.

The next day, Connie got a call from Joanne's mother asking where her daughter might be, and that she hadn't been to work in days, nor had she come home last night.

It was obvious that Joanne had become involved in something. But what? What changed her personality so drastically?

That evening, Joanne finally showed up at home. Connie went over to talk to her. When she stood in the doorway to the girl's room, she didn't recognize the person lying on the bed. She saw a limp body, clothes disheveled, hair dirty and ragged, and a pasty face.

The eyes, red and sunken, looked toward Connie.

"What do *you* want?" a rough voice said.

"I-I came to find out what's the matter," Connie said. "Can I help?"

"No." It sounded final. Joanne turned away.

"There has to be something wrong. You've changed."

Joanne sat up and glared at Connie. "Michael is mine."

"How do you know?"

"I was told."

"By whom? Did Mike tell you this?"

"No." She turned away again.

Connie didn't know how to respond. "Well, Joanne, why don't you go take a shower? That'll make you feel better. Then give me a call and we'll talk."

Joanne said nothing more.

About a half hour after Connie returned home, Mike called. "Get the guys," he said. "She's insane."

"What are you talking about? She's at home, taking a shower."

"She's HERE!"

The group rushed over, arriving in time to see her running out the door and into the woods. They went in to check on Mike.

"She's a maniac," Mike said, collapsing on the couch. There were scratches on his face and throat. "She clawed at me."

When they were sure Mike was okay, the friends went to Connie's house and sat on the front porch to discuss the problem. Screams interrupted them and Joanne came running onto the porch. She swore at them, talking gibberish. One of the bigger boys came up behind her to grab her. Her arm swung out and knocked him over the railing. Then she ran off.

The group lit after her. Connie went to Joanne's house to see if she had headed home. When the girl's mother answered the door, Connie said, "I've got to talk to you," and related what had just happened. The father sat nearby, buried in a newspaper.

The mother started to cry. "I don't understand."

"Are you sure you don't know what she's gotten involved with?" Connie asked.

"She spends a lot of time playing some parlor games, that's all."

"Like what?"

"I'll show you." She took Connie into the dining room and pointed to a Ouija board.

Just then Joanne came in. Her eyes were wide and glassy, her face pale.

"Joanne!" Connie said.

Joanne swore at her. "You! You are the cause of this!"

"Have you been using this Ouija board?" Connie asked, trying to hold her voice steady.

"They told me it's you!"

"Who told you?"

"They told me I had to go to Mike's. They told me he really loves me. They told me he can't see that because you are in the way!"

Connie turned to her friend's mother and said, "She needs help."

A few months later, Joanne's parents committed her to a mental institution. She has been there for over thirty years. The doctors have been unable to help her. They are not trained to look for demons.

Most people would like to think the Ouija board is nothing more than a game. We want answers in the midst of insecurities, and if we can convince ourselves that this alphabet board is merely a vehicle into our subconscious minds, then we can seek our answers and still feel safe.

But how safe is it really? According to Rev. Donald Page, a well-known clairvoyant of the Christian Spiritualist Church (a deceptive name for a church, since the Bible forbids spiritualism, i.e., consulting ghosts), using the Ouija board is "one of the easiest and quickest ways to become possessed."

Even those who see it as a psychological device warn of its dangers. Magician Danny Korem, who does not believe supernatural forces work through the Ouija, has stated, "I have seen, heard, and read, however, of many negative experiences that have entrapped people who have sought knowledge with a Ouija board. If you own a Ouija board or some similar diversion, my advice is to destroy it and never encourage others to tinker with such devices."[1]

Very often, the result of using a Ouija board is a deeper interest in the occult, as in my own experience. For others, such as Joanne, it leads to a life strongly influenced by demons: a life of obsession and sometimes even possession. This is why Joanne heard voices telling her what to do. This is where she got her superhuman strength. This is what changed her personality so drastically, so quickly and so incurably (psychologically speaking that is, since with Jesus nothing is incurable).

Kurt Koch, a Christian exorcist, refuted the theory that it's a harmless game in his book *Occult ABC*. His belief is that it ties into a supernatural force. He's said, "With the Ouija board, revelations from the hidden past and predictions about the future are made. These things could not possibly be stored in our subconscious minds."[2]

Other evidence points to dangerous supernatural forces: messages containing knowledge beyond that of the operator, frequent cases of the operator's personality being altered, and blindfold tests.

In 1914, Sir William Barrett reported that, when tested, the Ouija board worked well with the operators blindfolded, the alphabet rearranged and the board covered. He wrote, "Reviewing the results as a whole I am convinced of their supernormal character, and that we have here an exhibition of some intelligent, disincarnate agency, mingling with the personality of one or more of the sitters and guiding their muscular movements."[3]

These "disincarnate agencies" guide more than muscles. In 1933, newspapers sensationalized the story of a young girl who murdered her father because of a Ouija board. The girl's mother, Dorothea Irene Turley, had become an avid fan of the board. It prophesied where buried treasure could be found so that her husband, Ernest, would go looking for it while his wife secretly entertained a lover. Then Dorothea asked the board to choose between her men. It answered that her fifteen-year-old daughter, Mattie, who was Dorothea's partner on the board, should kill her father.

"Will the shooting be successful?" she asked it.

Yes.

"Will my husband die outright?"

No.

"What should Mattie use in the shooting?"

Shotgun.

"Will we inherit the ranch?"

Yes.

"Will the law get us?"

Do not fear the law. Everything will turn out all right.

After the murder, Mattie served six years in the Arizona State Industrial School. Her mother went to prison for three years.

Obviously, it was not God who spoke through the Ouija board. Was it Dorothea's subconscious, revealing a hidden desire to do away with her husband? Or had a supernatural force planted the ideas of unfaithfulness and murder?

Another famous case began in July of 1913 in Missouri. Two women worked the Ouija board while a third copied messages. The words came: "Many moons ago I lived. Again I come. Patience Worth my name. I would speak with thee."

In the weeks that followed, the entity claimed to have been a Puritan writer who had migrated to America, but who had been slain by an Indian before she could begin her literary career. Now, through Pearl Curran, who owned the Ouija board, she would finally get her chance at fame. She published a novel called *The Sorry Tale*, six more books, and thousands of poems and epigrams.

Patience Worth —what a name! A demon posing as a deceased writer could build a lot of trust in people by choosing such a wholesome-sounding name. Indeed, all across America people talked about Patience Worth. Some were inspired to contact their own dead literary geniuses. The popularity of using the Ouija board increased dramatically.

Was Patience Worth really a demon? It's doubtful Pearl Curran was the writer, since she claimed no literary talent and had left school during the eighth grade. We can rule out that Patience was a dead Puritan because, as we shall see in Chapter Six, when humans die, they cannot return to the living. Jesus used a parable to explain this in *Luke* 16:19-31. In the story, a rich man in Hell begs for someone to return from the dead to warn his brothers, but his request is refused.

If the dead cannot return to warn us about everlasting torment, can they return to write books? Of course not! So we're left with one conclusion: Patience Worth was a demon. Look at what she/it achieved, besides a by-line: More people became interested in the occult.

That's been the purpose behind the Ouija board from the beginning. The forerunner of the modern version goes back to about 540 B.C. Pythagoras and his sect held frequent seances using a table that rolled on wheels towards signs. It evolved, and in the second half of the nineteenth century, during America's first occult explosion, the spiritualist church adopted it as a religious artifact for communicating with the dead.

The credit for the modern version goes to two men from Maryland, E. C. Reichie and C. W. Kennard. They combined the alphabet board with the planchette and called it a *Witch Board*. Because people wanted to contact the dead, the product sold. In 1892, William Fuld, a foreman at the firm that produced it, bought the rights to it and recorded a patent. He renamed it the *Oriole Talking Board*, but the board informed both Fuld and Kennard that it should be called "Ouija": *Oui* from French and *ja* from German, both meaning "yes." Apparently, demons have good marketing skills.

Demand for the Ouija increased steadily. In 1899, William Fuld and his brother opened a factory in Baltimore. Although they had played with "spirit boards" since their youth, when asked if they believed in the board's power, William replied, "I'm no spiritualist. I'm a Presbyterian — been one ever since I was so high."

Patience Worth helped the Fulds become rich by popularizing communication with the dead. Then, on the eve of World War I, the Ouija informed William: "Prepare for big business." As soldiers died, sales skyrocketted. Wives and mothers wanted to talk to their lost loved ones. At least that's who they thought they were talking to. Demons know enough about our deceased loved ones to imitate them convincingly.

After the war, the Ouija's popularity continued. America had been hooked by this easy, seemingly safe access to the spirit world. In 1920, a writer for the *New York Tribune* reported that the Ouija had become a "national industry which bids fair to rival that in chewing gum."

The bombing of Pearl Harbor caused sales to soar again. Then, during the occult revolution of the 1960s, it gained the attention of Parker Brothers. Recognizing its profit potential, the company bought the rights to it in 1966. For the first time, it was packaged as a game. One year later, it outsold Monopoly.

Today, witches and others involved in the occult buy the Ouija for its effectiveness in communicating with the spirit world. A similar device, *The Angel Board* is growing in popularity among New Agers for the same reason.

Even if playing with the Ouija doesn't lead to deeper involvement in the occult, however, it is still a sin against God. Like swinging a pendulum for yes or no answers, reading tea leaves or consulting cards, it's a form of divination. It's also seeking the aid of "ghosts." God warns:

> *"Do not practice divination or soothsaying."*
> (*Lev.*19:26 NAB)
> *"For a sin like divination is rebellion."* (1 *Sam.*15:23 NAB)
> *"Let there not be found among you . . . a fortune-teller, soothsayer, charmer, diviner, or caster of spells, nor one who consults ghosts and spirits or seeks oracles from the dead."* (*Deut.* 18:10, 11 NAB)

We tend to disbelieve that dabbling in the occult is a sin, ignoring what God's Word says. Instead, we believe the same lie that Satan whispered into Eve's ear: "What God warns you about won't really happen. God just tells you to avoid this because it'll make you become like God

55

Himself. You are a better judge of what's best for you than He is!"

The sin in using a Ouija board is that we ask a question and expect a supernatural answer — but not from God. Why not look for answers we can trust? With the Holy Spirit in us, we don't need to turn to other spirits. Jesus tells us in *Luke* 11:9:

> *"Ask, and it will be given to you; search, and you will find; knock and the door will be opened to you."*

God does not give us the answers we seek through an alphabet board with a pointer. He uses the Bible, people, signs and wonders, the gifts of knowledge and wisdom, and innumerable other methods. But to hear His voice, we must first learn to distinguish it from others'. If we stop listening to the devil and start listening to God's Spirit, we can recognize the dangers.

For example, when the twelve-year-old daughter of a Christian pastor first encountered a Ouija board at a friend's birthday party, she didn't know what it was. She had never been exposed to the occult. Following the others into a dark room to play with the "game," she suddenly stopped.

"I can't go," she said.

"Why not, sweetheart?" the mother in charge asked. "It's just a game."

"No, it's wrong. I don't know why, but it's wrong. I can't do it."

Having been exposed only to God's ways, the girl had sensed the presence of evil. As a result, the host family wondered what made her different. They talked to her father and decided that they, too, wanted to be that close to the Lord.[4]

The demonic nature of the Ouija always reveals itself when in the presence of Christ. Matt was a teenager in a non-Christian family when his older brother got a Ouija board. They played with it a few times and nothing much happened, so his brother put it in the closet and never used it again.

Some time later, Matt gave his life to Christ. His brother went off to college, and Matt took over his bedroom. During the first night, as Matt drifted to sleep, he suddenly felt a heavy weight press down on his chest. It terrified him; he could hardly breath. It seemed like a huge, evil presence was trying to smother him. Matt tried to call Dad for help, but he couldn't get enough air into his lungs. With growing panic, he whispered, "Jesus!"

Instantly, the pressure disappeared.

The next night, Matt wondered if it would happen again. This time, he wanted to be on the alert for it. As he grew sleepy, the same evil weight besieged him and he immediately called for Jesus. The presence left.

Collecting his thoughts, he realized that the presence had seemed to come from the direction of the closet. He got out of bed to investigate. On the top shelf he found the forgotten Ouija board. Quickly, he broke it up and threw into the garbage can outside. Never again did he experience that heavy, evil attack on his chest.

---

* Not their real names

---

[1] Danny Korem & Paul Meier, *The Fakers*, Grand Rapids, MI: Baker Book House, 1980, pp. 70-71.

[2] Kurt Koch, *Occult ABC*, Grand Rapids, MI: International Publishers, n.d., p. 152.

[3] Sir William Barrett, *Proceedings of the American Society for Psychical Research*, 1914, p. 394.

[4] Rose Hall Warnke, *The Great Pretender*, Lancaster, PA: Starburst Publishers, 1985, pp. 160-161.

Chapter 4

Fortune Telling:
Psychic Gifts Come From God, Don't They?

Francine has been helping people with her crystal ball for fifteen years. Claiming to be a devout Catholic, she's said her ability to tell fortunes is a gift from God. "It's like being a gifted artist or a gifted pianist," she said. "This is my gift and I have to use it."

Julia*, a friend, once invited me to a fortune-telling party. When I told her I wouldn't go because occult powers come from Satan, she worried that maybe this party was a bad idea. So when the fortune teller talked to the guests about God, she felt very much relieved.

Although the only reason some psychics claim that their gifts come from God is to ease our minds, many truly believe it. Their reading rooms display more Christian symbols than many Christian homes, including crosses, pictures of Jesus and Mary, and statues of angels.

Jeane Dixon, one of the best-known modern psychics, said that her prophecies come from a well-developed intuition given to her by God. Edgar Cayce, another famous psychic, was a very religious church-goer who read the entire Bible often.

Is it possible that fortune tellers are doing the work of God? Could psychic powers be gifts from the heavenly Father, just like other talents? If we use them for good, how could they be satanic?

Let's ask this question: If psychic abilities come from God, then why does He forbid their use?

> *"Do not go to mediums or consult fortune tellers, for you will be defiled by them."* (*Lev.* 19:31 NAB)

God forbids it because it's a form of divination. Ouija boards, palmistry, card reading, crystal gazing, tea leaf reading, numerology, dowsing, pendulum-swinging, augury (interpreting signs and omens), color therapy, reading animal entrails, and so on, all use means other than God's ways to get help or information. The sin is seeking hidden knowledge without God. The sin is wanting to master the future to make it conform to our goals rather than trusting God and letting Him set the goals.

And, of course, there is the danger of opening the door to demons. Jennifer* discovered the fun of fortune telling at college. The girls in her dorm formed a Tarot Card Club. Then strange things began to happen.

Jennifer had left a basket of neatly folded and piled laundry on her bed before hurrying off to class. When she returned, she discovered that someone (or something) had thrown the clothes all around the room. Other times, things got mysteriously moved from where she'd put them. She said there were "just a lot of little things that weren't right." It happened to every member of the club. People couldn't find their homework. Sometimes found their term papers torn to shreds.

Jennifer did not want to believe that non-human forces had caused these disturbances, for then she would have had to stop playing with the Tarot cards. She preferred to think some person could get into each of the locked rooms with the sole purpose of moving things around.

Most people get very uncomfortable thinking their psychic talents might be evil, so they choose to believe their gifts come from God. But whether they know it or not, fortune tellers are agents of Satan —even if they use their gifts for good purposes. They propagate a forbidden practice, pass on the lie that God approves of it, and turn people away from God by encouraging them to depend on help from ungodly sources. God describes these tools of demons in the Bible (*Jer.* 14:14, 16 NJB):

> *The prophets are prophesying lies in my name; I*
> *have not sent them, I gave them no orders, I*

> *never spoke to them. Delusive visions, hollow*
> *predictions, daydreams of their own, that is*
> *what they prophesy to you. . . . I shall pour their*
> *own wickedness down on them.*

Furthermore, the Bible says that fortune telling provokes God's anger (2 *Chron.* 33:2, 6 NJB):

> *He did what is displeasing to Yahweh. . . . He*
> *practised soothsaying, divination and sorcery,*
> *and had dealings with mediums and spirit-*
> *guides. He did very many more things*
> *displeasing to Yahweh, thus provoking his*
> *anger.*

Therefore, no matter what we *want* to believe, if we involve ourselves with fortune telling, we are living a lie . 1 *John* 1:6 tells that we are liars if we say that we have fellowship with [God] while we walk in darkness.

The "gift" of foretelling the future, like any occult power, is a counterfeit of a true gift from God. There were servants of God in the Old Testament who foretold the future, and there are prophets today who get their knowledge from God. True Christian prophets are following Paul's advice (1 *Cor.* 14:1, 3) to us to ask for the gifts of the Holy Spirit.

Prophesying in the Christian sense does not always describe the future. We don't need to know the future. We can trust God, knowing that if we ask for His help, He will give us the best possible future.

Back in 1985, my husband and I asked God to help us sell our house. It should have been easy, because in those days, most houses sold in just a few weeks, sometimes even days. But when eight months passed with no buyers, I began to wonder if God really cared. I felt abandoned. I could have gone to a fortune teller to find out if and when we'd sell the house. I especially wanted to know if the new house we'd chosen would still be available. But I decided to trust God, overcome my impatience, and wait.

In the end, He honored my trust by working out the details so perfectly, it could only have happened because of Him. We even bought the house we had wanted, despite the interest of other buyers.

When God spoke through prophets in the Bible, He encouraged and instructed His people and foretold the future. Predictions were most common when the Israelites needed help awaiting their Messiah. Today we don't need predictions because the Messiah is in our midst and His second coming is prophesied sufficiently in the Bible. Whatever insecurities we have about the future can be turned over to Christ, enabling us to live the present in peace.

Jesus said in *Matt.* 6:25, 26, 33 (NJB):

> *I am telling you not to worry about your life. . .*
> *Look at the birds in the sky. They do not sow or*
> *reap or gather into barns; yet your heavenly*
> *Father feeds them. Are you not worth much*
> *more than they are? . . . Set your hearts on his*
> *kingdom first, and on God's saving justice, and*
> *all these other things will be given you as well.*

True prophecy is a manifestation of the Holy Spirit's presence to guide us in daily living, to enlighten the church, to set our hearts on His kingdom, and to assure us of our ultimate victory in Jesus Christ.

Fortune tellers do not do this. The Bible tells us in 1 *John* 4:1-3 (NJB):

> *My dear friends, not every spirit is to be*
> *trusted, but test the spirits to see whether they*
> *are from God, for many false prophets are at*
> *large in the world. This is the proof of the spirit*
> *of God: any spirit which acknowledges Jesus*
> *Christ, come in human nature, is from God, and*

> *every spirit which does not acknowledge Jesus is*
> *not from God, but is the spirit of Antichrist . . .*

In other words, we can discern if the source of a prophet's power comes from God or Satan by examining the fruits, i.e., the *results* of the use of the gift and the life of the person using it. Is Christ evident?

Francine, the Catholic fortune teller mentioned at the beginning of this chapter, shows where her loyalties are: "Even if the Church didn't accept me, I'd still do it. I have to do it."

Why does she *have* to do it? What forces control her that place themselves above the Church?

Francine's ability had developed at an early age. It did not come from growing closer to God. Visions began coming like flashes of light. (Remember, Satan disguises himself as an angel of light.)

It wasn't through Christ that she decided to start using her "gift." A spirit visited her in the night, looking like her mother, who had just died. (Demons know they can make us trust them when they disguise themselves as someone we love and miss.) The ghost told her she would make a living by being a psychic. The prediction became self-fulfilling a few months later when Francine quit her job to see clients.

Jeane Dixon also came upon her powers through the occult. Somewhere, sometime, each psychic must be exposed to the occult to be snagged by its powers. Demons cannot bestow their "gifts" on us unless a door is opened.

In Dixon's case, her mother took her at age eight to a gypsy fortune teller. The gypsy predicted she would have special powers, then gave her a crystal ball and fortune telling cards to seal her fate. Soon, Jeane received her first message.

"This voice comes to me frequently," she has said, "and I always listen to it."

When a person hears voices, we can usually assume

demon forces are at work (except in the case of chemical imbalances caused by certain diseases or drugs). God's voice sounds very different: it often comes from deep within our soul (although occasionally it is audible to the ears), it's an inner knowing that's filled with a sense of peace, it exudes His love, it offers biblically sound guidance, it focuses on His glory rather than our own, and it leads us closer to Christ.

The Bible offers these two ways to test the source of a prophet's voice (*Deut.* 13:1-4 RSV):

> *If a prophet . . . arises among you . . . and gives a sign or wonder, and the sign or wonder . . . comes to pass, and if he says to you, "Let us go after other gods . . ." you shall not listen to the words of that prophet.*

If the sign or wonder comes about: God's prophecies are one hundred percent accurate, always, because He is all-knowing and all-wise. Satan, on the other hand, does not know everything, although he wants us to believe he does. He can only guess at the future.

Jeane Dixon and other psychics have come up with some amazingly accurate predictions, but their failure rate is high. We forget their many false predictions because we like believing it is possible to see into the future.

If he says to you, "Let us follow other gods: It's also important to consider the philosophy that Jeane Dixon's predictions represent, i.e., the god she serves. None of Dixon's words lead people to the Lord. The times she has spoken of Christ, such as during the 1960s when she predicted His second coming and then revised it to mean the anti-Christ, she created confusion and took people's eyes off the Bible.

Look at what else she has represented: She's taught reincarnation. She's also preached that we should create a single universal religion created by combining all world religions; this would eliminate Christianity. The purpose of such a religion would be to solve humankind's problems. It denies that the solutions can be found in Jesus. Humans, the creators of this religion, become the Savior. Thus, Jeane Dixon's beliefs are saying we have no need for Christ at all.

"Any relationship between the God of the Bible and the ecumenical god of Mrs. Dixon is less than coincidental; it is nonexistent," wrote Gary North in *Unholy Spirits*.[1]

Edgar Cayce also worshipped a false god, the voice that diagnosed people's illnesses and prescribed remedies. His success rate was high, but, unlike predicting the future, here was a situation where the demons working behind the scenes could control the outcome.

Evidence of occult powers at work in his "ministry" abound. First of all, Cayce's remedies were usually unorthodox and not repeatable. They worked simply because spiritual forces did the healings. They often healed his patients' bodies, but they diseased their souls by leading them away from God and into the hands of demons.

Cayce was a devoutly religious man. He taught Sunday school and read the Bible from cover to cover many times over. How did he get so involved in the occult?

His grandfather practiced dowsing and psychokinetic abilities. Many people inherit demons from their families. Edgar had his first vision at age six. At thirteen, he saw a vision of a lady with wings. The next day, when he was struggling through a school lesson, he heard her voice say, "If you sleep a little, we can help you." After sleeping on his text book, he awoke with every fact memorized. This "gift" eventually faded. (Note: God's gifts do not fade except when we neglect to use them.)

As a faith healer, Cayce often questioned whether his ability came from God or the devil. But as he continued to use it, the demons' influence slowly eroded his thinking. After 1923, he stopped believing in the existence of Satan, resolving his dilemma: his "gift" **must** be from God.

At first he rejected the idea of reincarnation, rightfully acknowledging that it contradicts the principles of the Bible. But slowly he came to accept reincarnation, twisting Bible passages to back up his new belief. Eventually, he abandoned Christianity altogether. His psychic voice had become more important than the Bible.

His readings used Christian-sounding language to disguise their un-Christian content. They preached that All is One, that humans are co-creators with God and co-sovereigns of the universe. To quote Cayce's voice: "For ye are as a corpuscle in the body of God; Thus a co-creator with Him, in what ye think and in what ye do."

When we examine any psychic's belief systems, we can see similar deceptions about God. Clearly, this proves that fortune telling is satanic. Dr. John Newport explained this:

> Even if [knowing] the future were a form of inner sense, successful prophetic activity could be due to seers tuning into a mind powerful enough to know what will happen on the basis of analysis of all present factors that make up future events. Such a mind would have to be considerably more powerful than ours. It would have to integrate and analyze a vast number of factors. Thus the mind of God or minds of high-level supernatural beings would have to be involved.[2]

We have seen it is not the mind of God that the fortune teller taps into.

Dr. John Warwick Montgomery, a researcher into the occult, warned in his book *Principalities and Powers* about the ease with which demons overtake fortune tellers:

> Where, for example, the precognitive agent turns himself into, or allows others to turn

himself into, a "seer" who can pronounce on the nature of life and the meaning of the universe — precognition becomes a most dangerous quality. Moreover, used in this way, it opens the floodgates of the psyche to supernatural influences of the negative sort.[3]

M. Lamar Keene, a former medium, quit his profession because of the way mediums' lives usually ended. He wrote in *The Psychic Mafia*, "If I stayed in mediumship I saw only deepening gloom. All the mediums I've known or known about have had tragic endings. . . . Wherever I looked it was the same: mediums at the end of a tawdry life."[4]

Kurt Koch wrote that fortune telling is completely occultic because of the effect it has on people. He states that their religious lives reveal on the one hand an antagonism toward religion... a vicious critical attitude and an inability to pray or read the Bible if they are an atheistic type of person, while on the other hand the pious type reveals a self-righteousness, a spiritual pride...an insensitivity to the workings of the Holy Spirit.[5]

The effect it had on Katherine*, age forty-five, was devastating. Her husband had cheated on her and she suffered from deep depression and insomnia. Fortunately, she sought help at the Marian Center in central New Jersey, a Roman Catholic spiritual center known for its listening and healing ministries.

She poured out her miseries to Irene Huber, one of the center's founders, for an hour and a half. Then she mentioned she'd already gone for all kinds of help, none of which helped, including to a fortune teller.

"What?" Irene asked.

"What's wrong?" Katherine was surprised at the reaction.

"You've been to a fortune teller? What did she tell you?"

"That this was going to happen, that my husband was going to be unfaithful."

"Did you go to her once or several times?"

"I go to her quite frequently," Katherine said. "I find a lot of peace."

"If you find peace, how could you be depressed?"

"Oh, the peace lasts only a short time."

"How did she know your husband was going to be unfaithful?"

"I guess it came through her power."

Irene shook her head. "Do you realize what you're doing? Or what the Bible says about fortune telling?"

"Oh, but when I walk into that room, there's a big cross on the wall. And we call on Jesus' name."

"Really! And which Jesus is it that you call on?"

Katherine laughed nervously. "There's only one Jesus."

"It's not the same Jesus I know," Irene said.

"Oh, yes!"

"Oh, no. Go back to that fortune teller and ask her some questions. Ask her where she gets her power and authority from. Believe me, it's not from Jesus Christ. And ask her if she can say the Apostles' Creed."

Katherine agreed. The following week, she returned to the Center and told Irene: "I saw the fortune teller again."

"Did you have a session with her?" Irene asked.

"No. But she still charged me $45 for the questions I asked." She laughed.

"What did you get out of it?"

"I asked her what you told me to, and she said, 'Well, my power comes from *The Source.*'"

"Did you ask her what *The Source* was?"

"No. You know, Irene, the funniest thing happened. As I began to question her, she got very nervous. I don't know if that means anything."

"Of course it does, because she was being unmasked."

"And when I asked her to say the Apostles' Creed, she refused. She said she didn't have to prove anything, that her source was The Source of All Being. She said that if I doubted, the fortune telling wouldn't work anymore."

"Now do you believe her power does not come from Jesus Christ?"

"Who is the Jesus she talked about?"

"Satan."

"Oh."

"Katherine, now I know how to pray for you. You've exposed yourself to spirits of the occult, and they've gotten a foothold on your life. That's why medical treatment hasn't helped much. But I don't want you to be frightened. It doesn't mean you're possessed. It simply means we have to get rid of them. We're going to bind them and cast them away in the name of Jesus. First, what's your spiritual life like? I know it's very difficult to pray when you're depressed, but did you pray before?"

"No."

"Do you read Scripture?"

"Oh, yeah, I used to. I go to Mass on Sundays, but lately I haven't been able to do that."

"It's important that you continue reading Scriptures, get back to church, and begin to pray," Irene said. "For now, your prayer doesn't need to be anything more than five minutes of just saying: 'Jesus, Jesus, Jesus; I love you, Jesus, I trust you, Jesus.' That's prayer."

"That's prayer?"

"That's prayer! You can take it further later, but you've got to start building up your foundation. You've got to start bringing your spirit back up in order to heal the mind and body."

Then they prayed together—to cast out the spirits of insomnia, fear, fortune telling and occult involvement. Katherine felt no different, but she went home believing something must have changed.

Three days later she called Irene on the phone to tell her everything seemed to be going wrong — that it was just one thing after another. Irene explained to her that this is an indication of Satan's efforts to halt her spiritual progress. Continued prayer intercession was offered and further investigation into Katherine's difficulties. It was discovered Katherine's mother and grandmother had been involved in tea-leaf reading and other occult activities. Prayer was provided that present healing would also include heredity through the power and love of Jesus Christ, that Christ's blood — a reminder of His sacrifice on the cross — would protect Katherine.

"Anytime things are not as they should be," Irene told her, "ask Christ to cover you with His blood."

When Irene heard from her a week later, Katherine was completely normal. The depression had lifted, she could sleep through the night without medication, and her doctor couldn't believe she was the same woman.

---

* Not her real name

---

[1] Gary North, *Unholy Spirits*, Fort Worth, TX: Dominion Press, 1988, p. 191.

[2] Dr. John Newport, The *Biblical and Occult Worlds — A 20th Century Confrontation* tape series, Fort Worth, TX: Latimer House Publishing Co., 1973, "The Christian, Astrology and Prediction."

[3] John W. Montgomery, *Principalities and Powers*, Minneapolis, MN: Bethany Fellowship, 1973, pp. 125, 126.

[4] M. Lamar Keene, *The Psychic Mafia*, New York: St. Martin's Press, 1976, pp. 147, 148.

[5] Kurt Koch, *Between Christ and Satan*, Grand Rapids, MI: Kregel Publications, 1968, pp. 49, 50.

Chapter 5

Astrology:
It's Okay if I Don't Take It Seriously, Isn't It?

The only thing wrong with astrology, most people assume, is that it's scientifically implausible. So what's the harm in reading the daily horoscope in the newspaper? "I only read it to see how ridiculously generalized it is," I've been told.

"No demon is going to jump off the page and possess the reader who doesn't take it seriously," others say.

"What sign are you?" I often hear at parties.

"I don't believe in astrology," I reply.

"Well, I don't either, but there's no harm in talking about it."

They're always certain there's no harm. Yet astrology has become so well accepted that it's even the topic of seminars in churches and the subject of courses at church-sponsored colleges.

A Christian woman I know, who's a leader in her church, draws up detailed astrological charts for people.

"What about the Scriptures that tell us to have nothing to do with astrology?" I asked her once.

"They're misinterpreted," she answered. "They were written for the Israelites who were converting over to pagan religions. Astrology is just one of God's many methods of communicating with us. Proof of that is the astrologers who visited the baby Jesus."

Is she right? Let's take a closer look at the Magi from the East. They're sometimes referred to as magicians, astrologers, and Eastern mystics. Are they part of God's kingdom? Is that why they visited Jesus?

They were first of all Gentiles, i.e., non-Israelites. Their presence in the Christmas story shows us that Christ not only came to save the Jews, but the entire world. The Holy

Spirit inspired them to seek the Savior, even though their people had not been promised a Savior. They came to pay homage to the new ruler who would rescue Israel, even though they were not Israelites.

As some Bible translations call them, the magi were *wise men* from the East. *Today's English Version* translates it as "men who studied the stars." In those days, astrology and astronomy were one science. These men "had been waiting for a sign from God that would point them to the true source of divine guidance: God's living Word, made flesh in the Christ child," according to Rev. Gordon Dalbey of the United Church of Christ.[1]

Wise men or scholars of those days usually studied the sacred books and prophecies of their contemporaries. The ones that visited baby Jesus probably knew the famous oracle of Balaam: "A star shall come forth out of Jacob, and a scepter shall rise out of Israel" (*Num.* 24:17 RSV). Then, when they discovered an unusual star, they assumed that God was about to perform something wonderful in the earth. Remembering Balaam's prophecy, they set out on a pilgrimage to find out.

God can certainly manipulate His creations, in this case a star (or comet, as many contemporary astronomers suggest). Episcopal priest Dennis Bennett has pointed out that it is not wrong "to believe that God may use unusual activity or manifestations in the heavens to convey a message to man."[2]

But, the Star of Bethlehem had no significance as we understand the occult science of astrology today. It did not influence anyone's personality or predestine someone's future. It was, simply, an amazing sign.

Therefore, when astrologers paid homage to Jesus after His birth, they were not providing Biblical approval of horoscopes. So is astrology one of God's methods of communicating with us?

God wants us, first and foremost, to seek His guidance from the Bible, His holy, divinely-inspired Word. God's

Word can keep us on the right road and prevent us from stumbling. It can prepare us for the future and help us make decisions. Of course, if we rely only on our own understandings and perceptions, we can easily make the mistake of misinterpreting what we read. Correct interpretations can only be made through the inspiration of the Holy Spirit combined with the guidance of Church authorities who are relaying what has been passed down by the Holy Spirit from the beginning.

Does astrology really work? God's prophecies are always accurate.

Scientifically speaking, there is no statistical evidence to back up astrologers' claims. Such was the finding in 1961 of Paul Couderc, an astronomer at the Paris Observatory. After examining the horoscopes of 2,817 musicians, he found no correlation between their musical talents and their zodiac sign. Astrology is not capable of predicting or governing musical talent—or any other talent or career.

Another researcher tracked 550 astrological predictions for a year to determine their accuracy. Only 24 of them (less than five percent) proved true.

We have to wonder why people let so many false predictions rule their lives. Even the heads of corporations and the wife of a U.S. president have relied on them. Business executives have depended on the advice of astrologers to determine who to hire and how to invest. There are at least 100 "financial astrologers" in America, charging $10,000 and up for corporate consultations. In 1994, according to astrologer Henry Weingarten, he and his colleagues influenced $14 billion in investment funds.

Second, astrology is based upon the ancient misconception that the planets and sun revolve around the earth. It was also created before scientists discovered Uranus, Neptune and Pluto.

Third, when twins are born, they should, according to astrology, lead identical lives or have identical—or nearly identical—personality traits. But they don't.

Fourth, since the original astrologers lived close to the equator, they did not take into consideration people who live in Alaska, Norway, Finland and other high latitudes where the zodiac signs do not even appear for the same length of time!

Fifth, casting a horoscope based on the moment of birth does not take into account that a person's heredity is determined nine, eight, or even ten months earlier at conception.

Sixth, the constellations have shifted about thirty degrees over the past 2,000 years, but no adjustment by astrologers has been made to compensate for it.

Seventh, there are so many different systems of astrology, you could go to two astrologers and receive two opposite predictions! For example, just before President Kennedy's assassination in 1963, three prominent astrologers in Germany read his charts. One predicted he'd be re-elected, one said he'd die, and the third said he'd retire due to illness in the summer of 1964.

So if there is so much evidence against astrology working, why do so many people believe in it? Probably they feel a **need** to believe in it. Their reasons include:

1. The future is so uncertain, especially today, that we want help in forging our way through the present.

2. We want meaning for our lives when so much else seems meaningless.

3. We want to feel like an important part of the universe.

4. Astrology offers a short cut to self-knowledge and solutions for our problems.

5. It's easier to believe that the reason you're having a bad day is because it's in your stars, rather than take the responsibility of making it better.

Another reason people believe in astrology is that it

does work—once in a while. Not often enough to convert the skeptics, but definitely enough to hook the horoscope reader into letting it rule his or her life.

Here's how.

When life goes smoothly and we feel self-sufficient, we take little interest in astrology. Then life falls apart and we find ourselves in the midst of change. A lover rejects us, a job is threatened by layoffs, illness strikes, or some plan for our future gets sidetracked. Suddenly, we're faced with: What's going to happen to me?

The astrology column beckons us with its promise of easy answers. As we read it, we discover that our decisions are already made for us. It may seem generalized at first, but didn't that one prediction come true? We begin to look for others coming true. Given enough information, we find ways the horoscopes match our experiences.

For example, if we read that we'll hear from a long-lost friend, we start thinking about that childhood pal in Arkansas. Soon, our curiosity about what she's been doing inspires us to call her. The horoscope was right, but it was only a self-fulfilled prophecy (which is why internationally-respected psychologist Dr. Joyce Brothers has criticized astrology).

Gradually, we become dependent on astrology as it seduces us into believing that everything is predestined. We stop taking responsibility for our actions because we think we have no control over our destiny. We think our fate has already been determined. We become fatalistic.

Then, when our horoscope predicts disaster, we stay home instead of going to work or to a friend's house. And we do nothing at home because accidents can happen on the stairs or while ironing or cleaning. Worse than that, by believing that disaster will happen, we can unconsciously place ourselves into situations that cause disaster.

When we trust astrology, it becomes a counter-religion. C. S. Lewis, in his spiritual autobiography, *Surprised by Joy,* called the desire to pry into the future a disease. "It is a spiritual lust," he wrote. "And like the lust of the body, it has the fatal power of making everything else in the world seem uninteresting while it lasts."

Spiritual lust is a good description of astrology. It is an intense desire that falls short of true love. It makes astrology a false god that we ravenously pursue when, in fact, we should be loving and trusting the God Who truly loves us. We become preoccupied with devotion to the creation and overlook the love of the Creator.

Because God always cares about us, even when we don't love Him, and because only He is all-wise and all-knowing, He is the only reliable source of information about the future. When Daniel interpreted King Nebuchadnezzar's dream after astrologers had failed, he said that only God correctly reveals secrets and makes known what will happen in latter days (*Dan.* 2:28).

The Bible tells us over and over again that our personality and potential are determined by our relationship with the heavenly Father, not by our relationship with stars and planets. The stars reveal the glory of God in that He created them. But when we allow our lives to be ruled by these stars, we obey them as if they were gods. That's why astrology is idolatry.

Idolatry was the purpose of astrology since its beginning.

The first known astrologers were the Chaldeans and Babylonians, around 3,000 B.C. They recorded data about the sun, moon and those "stars" that moved — the planets. Because the planets travelled through the sky, people believed they were supernatural beings, gods to be worshipped. That's why, to this day, they bear the names of gods. In order to learn the intentions of these gods, the ancient people developed a method of interpreting their movements.

Later, the Greeks and Romans refined the system. They thought that each person reflected the pattern of the heavens at the moment of his or her birth. Further, they thought that the changing patterns influenced the person's life to such an extent that one could describe the condition of that person at any given time by examining the positions of the planets.

During the seventeenth century, when Copernicus and Galileo proved that the sun is the center of the solar system, astrology lost its following. Only recently, with the rise of the New Age movement, has it become popular again. Proof of its acceptance into the mainstream of our society is Linda Goodman's *Sun Signs*, which became the first astrology book to make *The New York Times* best-seller list. First published in 1968, by 1995 it sold more than five million copies.

Do we believe there are gods in the stars today? If not, where do we think their power to influence us comes from? True, we are physiologically influenced by the sun and moon: The sun tans us, gives us Vitamin D, and causes cancer; the moon's gravity creates minute tides in the water content of our bodies, sometimes contributing to certain moods. But we cannot use these celestial objects to predict human events. And the stars and planets have even less effect on us.

However, a 1990 Gallup poll showed that twenty-four percent of Americans believe that the stars and planets do affect our behaviors and life-events. A study made by Professor Jon D. Miller of Northern Illinois University, vice president of the Chicago Academy of Sciences, revealed that only twelve percent of Americans believe astrology is "not at all scientific." Forty-eight percent believe this to varying lesser extents.

The remaining people surveyed believe that astrology has some plausibility. Of these, five percent say they completely rely on what the stars predict—that's about nine million people who are absolutely convinced that astrology is valid and dependable.

Astronomer Dr. Carl Sagan has found that astrology is popular because too little attention is given to science. He told science writers at Cornell University, "Every newspaper in America has a daily astrology column, with one or two exceptions. Virtually no newspaper in America, as far as I know, has a daily science column." Sagan expressed alarm over astrology's popularity in the media because "it encourages the antithesis of scientific thinking."

Sagan said he wants horoscopes removed from newspapers, or at least given a disclaimer stating that astrology has no scientific basis. However, his reasons go beyond the damage it does to science. He pointed out that astrology "shares with sexism and racism the idea that you can divide the human community into a few slots, and you can decide about people by knowing which of the twelve slots they happen to fit into."

Millions of people fail to understand this. They believe that astrology works due to a perceived all-encompassing unity of the cosmos. They believe that we are one with nature and with God, that "all is one." But this is simply not true. The Bible clearly rejects the idea. God is the Creator, not the creation. His power is **supreme** above all, and, rather than making us one with nature, He has put us in authority over it, as seen in *Genesis* 1:26 (RSV) where He said:

> *Let them* [mankind] *have dominion over the fish of the sea, and the birds of the air, over the cattle, and over all the earth, and over every creeping thing that creeps upon the earth.*

The "all is one" philosophy is straight from Satan because he was the first to try to make creation (himself) equal to the Creator. This is one reason astrology can be called satanic.

The stars and planets are not masters over us. Even the moon with its gravitational pull is not to be our master. Though statistically there are more crimes and accidents during the period from three days prior, to three days after a full moon, a prayer to God can overcome whatever moods or "lunacy" the moon might cause.

Any effect the zodiac has on us is purely psychological. It makes us fatalistic, leaving us without hope. Why strive for goals if the stars may work against us? Why make decisions if we have no free will? Why try to improve our lives if the future's not ours to create? Astrology robs us of hope, and where there is no hope, there is fear.

Have you ever imagined what fear might look like? The following true story gives us an example of one form of fear.

A woman who had been involved in astrology went to Irene Huber of the Marian Center seeking help for overwhelming fear. She was afraid to get in her car and afraid to get out. She panicked about leaving home. She feared the roads and stores. Her anxieties were ruining her life. Fear literally controlled her.

After Irene questioned the woman to learn all she could about the cause of the problem, she and two other women began to pray for her. In the name of Jesus Christ, they asked for release from any occultic spirit, such as astrology. They asked Jesus to give her His victory in her life. As they continued praying, Irene saw something unusual in her mind's eye. It was so unusual, she didn't mention it to the others.

When it was time to leave, the woman seemed a changed person. She smiled and there was a bounce in her step. For the first time in too long, she could open the door and enjoy the sunshine of the outdoors.

After she was gone, one of those who had prayed for her said, "You know, I don't know whether to say anything or not, but I saw something."

Irene looked at her. "Really? I did, too."

"Well, what did you see?"

"I think I just have a very vivid imagination," Irene

answered.

The third woman also confirmed a vision.

They all stared at each other with growing excitement. Each had seen the same vision at the same moment. Black, furry creatures emerging from the woman. All three women had seen the creatures fly across the room to the doors and windows and scurry away.

"I can't explain it," Irene said later. "That woman was delivered of fear. What those things were and why there were so many, I can't explain. I don't know if we actually saw demons of fear, but all three of us saw the same thing at the same time. That's why I know it had to be real."

A word of caution is due here. Getting rid of occult influences and obsessive forces such as fear should not be taken lightly. There is a danger in relying solely on prayer. Medical and psychological treatments should not be overlooked where those needs seem obvious. However, sometimes medical and psychological methods are not enough if the occult is involved. Spiritual problems are most effectively dealt with if spiritual help is included in treatment.

There is also a need for caution in attempting to deal with strictly occultic forces on our own. Evil spirits and demons are everthing their name conjours up to us, and we may be no match with them on a one-on-one basis. Binding and casting out spirits is one of the gifts our Creator has given us to deal with the forces of evil in the world. But we are still mere mortals. We can not cure or heal. God Heals. We cannot dispense graces. They come from God. In serious circumstances, we should also seek the direction of a priest and the power of the Church and her Sacraments. For the woman who came to the Marian Center seeking assistance, spiritual help—in the form of intense prayer—made all the difference.

Why and how do we put ourselves into the hands of demons? Dr. John Newport has warned:

Astrology as part of the occult has often

been an instrument of Satan in leading people into the slavery of fear and despair of uncontrollable forces. We expose ourselves to the possibilities of satanic enslavement when we become actively involved in serious astrology.[3]

Those who do not become enslaved by fear through astrology become slaves nonetheless. They are held captive by the cosmic forces that they believe determine their destiny. They are enslaved by what they think is an outside force controlling their lives. They are imprisoned by fatalism, convinced that they cannot change or correct what lies ahead.

If we have this attitude, we drift aimlessly along, settling for less than the best, never reaching our fullest potential, never even coming close to the wonderful supernatural love of Almighty God and all the gifts He wants to bestow on us. As long as the stars rule us, we miss experiencing the victorious faith that overcomes the world, as described in *John* 5:4,5 (RSV):

> *This is the victory that overcomes the world, our faith. Who is it that overcomes the world but he who believes that Jesus is the Son of God?*

God gives us freedom, not bondage. He deliberately limited His control over us so we could exercise free will. But we often choose astrology or other occult activity instead of Him. That is idolatry.

Idolatry is a sin against our Creator. But practicing astrology is also a sin against ourselves. It keeps us from becoming the very best that God wants for us.

God is more powerful than any of His creations, more powerful than a planetary alignment that might tell us we're destined for tragedy or for a certain type of career or love life. If we seek Him earnestly, we can receive His power to change tragedies into triumphs, to find the career that is truly right for us, and to marry the best choice of spouse or to heal broken relationships.

God has a plan for our lives that's better than anything the stars might predict. It's the best plan possible. And what makes trusting God even more exciting is that whenever we stray from the best, we can turn to Him for help. He will steer us back to the best road. God assures us of this in *Jeremiah* 29:11 (TLB):

> *I will come and do for you all the good things I have promised, and bring you home again. For I know the plans I have for you, says the Lord. They are plans for good and not for evil.*

In the next verses of this Scripture, God tells us how to grab hold of those plans (*Jer.* 29:12-14 (NJB):

> *When you call to me and come and pray to me, I shall listen to you. When you search for me, you will find me; when you search wholeheartedly for me, I shall let you find me.*

God not only will but *wants* to change every circumstance in our lives into good. He wants to lead us from glory to glory, helping us through the bad times, lifting us higher than we've ever been before. It's no wonder, then, that God inspired Paul to write in *Colossians* 2:8 (NAB):

> *See to it that no one deceives you through any empty, seductive philosophy that follows mere human traditions, a philosophy based on cosmic powers rather than on Christ.*

And in *Isaiah* 47:13,14 (NJB) we find God warning:

> *You have had many tiring consultations: let the astrologers come forward now and save you, the star-gazers who announce month by month what will happen to you next. Look, they are like wisps of straw, the fire will burn them up. They*

> *will not save their lives from the power of the flame.*

Only through Jesus Christ can we be saved. His power is greater than any other power, including the "power of the flame," which refers to the fire of judgment, the place where Satan abides.

Daniel, in the days of ancient Israel's Babylonian exile, proved time and again that God's power is far superior to astrology. King Nebuchadnezzar had been disturbed by a bad dream, so he summoned his astrologers and soothsayers.

"This is my firm resolve," he commanded. "If you cannot tell me what I dreamt and what it means, I shall have you torn limb from limb."

"Nobody in the world could explain the king's problem," they answered.

Enraged, the king ordered all the sages to be put to death. But Daniel, who'd been forced into service at the royal court, asked the king to give him the opportunity to reveal the interpretation.

With permission granted, Daniel went to his friends and asked them to help him pray for the explanation. During the night, God revealed the mystery.

The next day, Daniel stood before the king.

"Can you tell me what I dreamt and what it means?" the king asked.

"The mystery about which the king has inquired, the wise men, enchanters, magicians and astrologers could not explain. But there is a God in heaven who reveals mysteries," answered Daniel, who then described the dream and its meaning.

Nebuchadnezzar was so impressed, he fell down and worshipped Daniel. "Truly your God is the God of gods and Lord of kings and a revealer of mysteries," he said. And he made Daniel chief of all the sages.

Later, the king had another mysterious dream. Again

the astrologers and soothsayers failed to interpret it, and again Daniel's God revealed the answer.

Years passed, and Crown Prince Belshazzar was given authority in Babylon. He threw a great party for a thousand of his lords and their women. After imbibing too much wine, he asked for the gold and silver vessels that had been plundered from God's temple in Jerusalem. As they drank from them and praised their gods, suddenly a hand appeared and wrote an indecipherable message in the plaster of the wall.

Belshazzar screamed for his astrologers and soothsayers, but none of them could read the writing or guess what it meant. The sages remembered Daniel's ability and recommended he be summoned. Daniel looked at the writing and knew exactly what it meant. He was far wiser than the sages because he served God instead of the stars. God gave him the answers he sought.

These stories can be found in the Old Testament book of Daniel, chapters two through five. Throughout the Bible, there are stories of God's superiority over all powers of the occult. They await our discovery.

---

[1] Gordon Dalbey, "The Beast in the Beauty of the Stars," *Christian Herald*, Sept., 1985.

[2] ibid.

[3] Dr. John Newport, The *Biblical and Occult Worlds--A 20th Century Confrontation* tape series, Fort Worth, TX: Latimer House Publishing Co., 1973, "The Christian, Astrology and Prediction."

Chapter 6

Channelling: Out on a Fragile Limb

At New Age conventions, where you can find booths and seminars and books and people covering every imaginable occult phenomenon and promise, the most successful booths are those where spirits are channeled through human mouthpieces to "counsel" customers. People throng to them for help on matters ranging from money woes to confusing relationships, from job direction to spiritual direction.

Channeling has become the biggest fad in the occult world. Now you can turn your body and your life over to the spirit of an intelligent being and have him dispense words of wisdom to others. In exchange for this possession, the channeled spirit offers answers and wealth and fame. In an insecure world, multitudes swarm to this kind of supernatural power, relying on it for all kinds of important decisions, including those that affect their eternal lives.

The "guides" who speak through channelers claim to be the spirits of people who died long ago, gods, and people of ancient civilizations, extraterrestrials, Native American Indians, Elvis Presley, disciples of Jesus, Jesus Himself, and even a group of dolphins.

Voices from beyond have written books. *Jonathan Livingston Seagull* was dictated to Richard Bach by a spirit who appeared as a bird. The book topped the best-seller list for two years. Even Christians have found the tale inspiring. It seems to refer to Jesus Christ and Heaven and self-improvement. But it subtly promotes reincarnation and self-deification.

Ruth Norman, who founded the *Unarius Academy of*

Sciences in 1975, produced over ninety books that entities "wrote" through her. The organization's advertising copy says: "All texts and teachings were transmitted from Higher Beings on Advanced Planets." They include stories about life on Venus, Napoleon Bonaparte's reincarnations, the return of Atlantis, New Age preachings by dead scientists, unphotographable spiritual planets inhabited by "messengers," and underground cities on Mars that her late husband astral-projected himself to. According to Charles Spiegel, head of the academy since the 1993 death of Mrs. Norman, 500,000 people worldwide had purchased Unarius literature by 1994.

The central purpose of Unarius is to prepare for the arrival of a thousand scientists from outer space in the year 2001 (originally, Mrs. Norman had been certain that they'd arrive in 1976). They will make a brief stop in the Bermuda Triangle and then land in thirty-three ships on the Unarius property.

Mrs. Norman called herself "a Channel for the Light Forces of this world" and promised to turn all her readers into channelers. "In your search for a channel, why settle for anything less than the best?" her ads pitched.

Today's interest in spirit guides took off with the *Seth Speaks* books in the 1970s. Their author, Jane Roberts, became possessed by Seth after playing with a Ouija board. A million readers have purchased her books.

Channeling's popularity grew gradually, but exploded when actress Shirley MacLaine published her 1983 auto-biography and starred in the subsequent 1987 TV movie of the same name, *Out on a Limb*.

Merv Griffin responded to the public's curiosity on his television talk show by interviewing MacLaine's favorite spirit, Ramtha, channeled by Mrs. J. Z. Knight. People across America tuned in to hear this supposedly 35,000-year-old conqueror of Atlantis. Ramtha told the audience, "What is termed God is within your being. . . . And that which is called Christ is within your being." This message is commonly preached by channeled spirits.

However, there is deception in Ramtha's words. We find a clue to it in his next statement: "And when you know you are God, you will find joy."

Does the Spirit of God within you tell you there's something wrong here? It should, for we are not God. The truth is, when you *find* God, that is when you find joy. Jesus said in *John* 15:10, 11 (NJB):

> *If you keep my commandments you will remain in my love. . . . I have told you this so that my own joy may be in you and your joy be complete.*

It is pure deception to say, "When you know you are God, you will find joy." When we believe we are God, we see no need for Christ the Savior. We deny ourselves the opportunity to receive His joy. Instead, we live in the everyday emotions of this world — fear, greed, jealousy, disappointment, etc. Any joy offered through the occult is short-lived. God our Father made it possible for us to have lasting joy by offering us His greatest gift of love: God the Son came to earth as a man and traded His divine life for our sinful lives. He took all our fear, greed and other problems to the cross with Him. It is He who should be our spiritual guide, as is written in 1 *Timothy* 2:5, 6 (NJB):

> *For there is only one God, and there is only one mediator between God and humanity, himself a human being, Christ Jesus, who offered himself as a ransom for all.*

When we put our trust in this truth, Christ comes to us and fills us with His own supernatural joy.

Then why has communicating with spirits become so popular? Books about channeling outsell all other occult topics. People flock by the hundreds to expensive seminars to listen to channelers. In the Los Angeles area alone, there are more than a thousand active channelers.

People have eagerly paid $300 to hear Shirley MacLaine speak. MacLaine's reason for this price: $100 for the mind, $100 for the body, and $100 for the spirit.

J. Z. Knight was able to build a multi-million-dollar dream mansion thanks to public fascination with channeling. She's charged $400 to $1500 *per person* for her seminars. Ramtha, who first came to Knight while she was playing with crystal pyramids, has attracted seven hundred to eight hundred people at a time by telling them, "You need answers. I am here to answer you."

Many customers become emotionally dependent on consultations with psychics, according to Detective Tom Henton of the Los Angeles Police Department's Bunco Unit. "It's very common (for them) to spend $10,000, $20,000, $25,000" on their addiction to occult advisors. He warns that many of the psychics are frauds whose only special gift or power is the ability to listen to people's problems and pick up on clues to make their advise seem supernaturally on-target. His findings are confirmed by Stephen Kaplan, executive director of the *Parapsychology Institute* of America, based in Elmhurst, N.Y.

"People should be very skeptical of this field," he has said. "It's only about ninety-five percent fake. Most of the people who try to make money in it aren't real."

Interest in spirits does not stop with advise-seeking. Haunted houses have become tourist attractions. Newspapers and other news media carry stories of hauntings, especially around Halloween. Television shows and movies depict ghosts with increasing frequency because the public is so fascinated by the supernatural.

According to Marcello Truzzi, professor of sociology at Eastern Michigan University and director of Ann Arbor's *Center for Scientific Anomalies Research*, "If you told people fifty years ago that there was a ghost in a house, everyone would ooh and aah and stay away. You tell people now, and everyone wants to spend the night there."

Spirits speaking to us from beyond seem to offer

assurance that life does not come to a meaningless end. However, listening to them cannot give us life after death. Only Jesus can. *Hebrews* 2:14, 15 (TLB) tells us:

> [Jesus] *became flesh and blood . . . for only as a human being could he die and in dying break the power of the devil who had the power of death. Only in that way could he deliver those who through fear of death have been living all their lives as slaves to constant dread.*

Our society has become biblically illiterate. We don't know much of what God's Word says, so we underestimate the abundance of gifts He wants to give us. We also underestimate the power of demons. It is no wonder that in our desperation to know that death is not final, we listen to the false hopes offered by channelers. But the Bible warns in 2 *Peter* 2:3 (NJB):

> *In their greed they will try to make a profit out of you with untrue tales. But the judgment made upon them long ago is not idle, and the destruction awaiting them is forever on the watch.*

Emanuel Swedenborg, an eighteenth-century mystic who's been called the first spiritualist, wandered through the spirit world conversing with those he encountered. Even he concluded, "When spirits begin to speak with a man, he must beware that he believe nothing that they say. For nearly everything they say is fabricated by them, and they lie: for if they are permitted to narrate anything, as what heaven is and how things in the heavens are to be understood, they would tell so many lies that a man would be astonished."[1]

Why would the spirits of dead humans lie? It seems like more people tell fibs in the afterlife than they do here on Earth—assuming they are people. Demons, on the other hand, are most assuredly liars. Obviously the spirit world is full of demons, and we cannot trust what they tell us through channelers, Ouija boards or any other means.

However, we are quite vulnerable to accepting lies as truths unless we use the Bible to help us discern between the two. We are vulnerable to the spirits who offer words of wisdom designed to pull us away from the truth of God.

I believed the lies when I was fifteen years old and holding frequent seances. On one occasion, a spirit claimed it needed our help. He said his name was Jonathan Damien and that he'd died in France in 1820. He also revealed he'd been watching us for some time before deciding to contact us.

He wanted us to help him find his wife, Maria. This is the story he told us: Maria had been orphaned as a child when her parents were murdered by ten hired men. Later, after marrying Jonathan, she discovered that these men were friends of his. In revenge, Maria set their apartment on fire while the men visited, accidentally also killing her husband. When she realized what she had done, she committed suicide. Now, Jonathan wanted to be reunited with her, but the ten evil men had taken her captive in the afterlife because of her deed.

Suddenly, our medium twitched nervously. Maria took over her body, having just escaped those men, and pleaded for our help. We vowed our assistance, but there was nothing we could do to keep the invisible men away from her. Our medium snapped out of her trance. The men had snatched Maria back.

We actually believed this bizarre story. It seemed so real as we watched one personality, then another, possess our friend's body. But was it real? Is it possible there are spirits in need of our help?

Three months after that seance, I attended a lecture at the local high school featuring Hans Holzer, internationally known as the "Ghost Hunter." He has written something close to ninety books on the subject.

He claimed, "With the majority of people, [the] inner self—also referred to as the soul—will drift out into the next dimension, which some call the spirit world. The problem comes when somebody passes, or rather doesn't pass, from one state to the other due to emotional turmoil, sudden shock, trauma, great sickness, or some other form of inhibiting factor that keeps the person in an unnatural state in the physical world. That's what ghosts are.

"For them, time stands still. . . . They become paranoid at times, psychotic at others. They are never quite themselves because they are not able to understand their own predicament."

That last statement is very revealing, for it's a good description of demons. Time standing still would be eternity, where there is no time-line as we know it. Demons are most assuredly paranoid and psychotic. And they do indeed fail to understand their own predicament, because they keep denying that Christ has already broken their power through His crucifixion and resurrection and that Christ will completely defeat them in the end.

Holzer continued, "Feel sorry for those in that in-between stage, but don't be scared. They can't do a damn thing to you. Somebody has to reach out to them and help them go on."

Is there a reason to be scared? Can they do "damn" things to you? The Bible shows us the truth about life after death and that there is indeed eternal life. But in order to get into the heavenly house God has built for us, we must do something ourselves. We need to listen to the words of Jesus and believe in the One who sent Him

Only Jesus can open the door to our house in Heaven. Channeling with spirits cannot get us in; it neither teaches Jesus' words nor helps us believe in God (*John* 5:44 NJB):

> *How can you believe, since you look to each*

> *other for glory and are not concerned with the*
> *glory that comes from the one God?*

Channeling glorifies spirits. It does not glorify the Holy Spirit. Therefore, yes, "ghosts" *can do* damn things to us. They can keep us from receiving eternal life in Heaven by convincing us to believe we don't need Jesus.

What about this "in-between" stage Holzer mentioned? Is there such a place? Second *Peter* 2:9, 10 (NJB) says no, it's impossible, because God has a different plan for those who reject His Son:

> *The Lord is well able to . . . hold the wicked for*
> *their punishment until the Day of Judgment,*
> *especially those who follow the desires of their*
> *corrupt human nature and have no respect for*
> *the Lord's authority.*

Therefore, there can be no half-way zone from which the spirits of the dead can speak to the living. So then, just who or what haunts houses and visits us in seances?

People who reject Jesus are imprisoned in the afterlife by their own choice. They have separated themselves from God. Anyone whose name cannot be found in God's Book of Life — anyone who has rejected life with Jesus — will be hurled into the burning lake of the second death along with Satan and the other demons (*Revelation* 20:14, 15).

On the other hand, all those who choose to love Jesus follow Him into everlasting life in His Father's kingdom.

There is no "in-between."

And there is no going back from any kind of afterlife to speak to those in the physical world. Jesus' parable in *Luke* 16:29-31 makes this clear. The rich man in Hades (the place of imprisonment where people await Final Judgment) begs for someone to return from the dead to give his brothers warning "so that they do not come to this place of torment too." But his request is denied: "They will not be convinced even if someone should rise from the dead." Jesus rose from the dead, but still people don't believe His message.

Since the spirits we contact cannot be dead people imprisoned in Hades, are they people who died believing in Christ? We can answer that by considering the personalities of these spirits. Do they act like people who know Jesus? Do they have peace? Do they tell us how to find everlasting life in Jesus? Do they glorify God?

Definitely not! Ghosts do not live in peace. Ghosts never speak of Jesus as the way to salvation. Ghosts never glorify God. "Jonathan" and "Maria" definitely had no peace.

So, who are we contacting if we fool with the spirit world? There is only one conclusion. We've ruled out the spirits of people who died rejecting Jesus. We've ruled out the spirits of people who died loving Jesus. We know that angels would not lead us away from God. There is only one type of spiritual being left: demons.

Channeled spirits are certainly not any of Jesus' disciples—or Jesus Himself—as some claim to be. Look at where they lead us: not to the Christ who deepens our relationship with God the Father; not to the Christ who inspires us to study His Word in the Bible; not to the Christ who promises everlasting salvation.

No, they lead us away from that Christ and His love. They lead us to reject Jesus, the only divine Son of God our Father, Who died to set us free from sin and bring us to eternal life in Heaven. They lead us to the aloneness of hell and the Final Judgment. Who wants us to stay away from the Bible and its message of supernatural love? Who wants to keep us out of Heaven?

Demons! Any method we use to communicate with the spirit world exposes us to demons.

It should be noted, however, that this does not include asking for prayer support from saints (i.e., people who love God and live in His kingdom) who have died. Since all Christians, both living and dead, belong to Christ's family, we have a connection to the Communion of Saints who have left this world. Through this connection, we can communicate our love and our need for their prayers. When we do, however, we are not talking with them; that would be dangerous because demons can disguise themselves as our deceased loved ones. We are merely sharing our love and sending our prayer requests through Jesus and receiving their love and the help of their powerful intercessions.

On the other hand, when we try to enter the spirit world ourselves or hold conversations with spirits, we put ourselves at great risk. Abbot David Geraets, O.S.B., who ministers to people affected by the occult, has said, "I've prayed with a number of people who have encountered evil spirits when entering the spiritual world with a meaningless mantra. The same things often occur to those who use a countdown system, active imagination, or other techniques without Jesus."[2]

Twenty-three-year-old Rick* sought spiritual help after several years of Transcendental Meditation (TM). Satan had grabbed hold of his mind through a mantra. Rick became obsessed by fear and guilt. Voices told him he could find peace through drugs. During his good moments, he became very despondent because he knew he had no control over what was happening to him.

He was advised to get rid of everything he had used during his meditations, and to also identify his mantra so that prayer could be offered to overcome it. But Rick could not initially bring himself to reveal it fearing it would bring him harm. The counselors assured him that Jesus was stronger than any mantra, than any spirit, and could free him.

For those not familiar with the term, a *mantra* is a Hindu phrase or word repeated over many times—as a sort of prayer—to unite one to the spiritual world. It is also the name of an ancient pagan deity. Mantras are links to the demons of TM. Rick could not be set free from his imprisonment through TM until the power of his mantra was broken.

Mantras cause problems by calling on demons, and their purpose is to lead us away from worship of God and lead us into worship of self. Shirley MacLaine said as much in her book, *Dancing in the Light*. Notice how use of mantras encourages self-deification:

> The ancient Hindu vedas claimed that the spoken words *I am,* or *Aum* in Hindu, set up a vibrational frequency in the body and mind that align the individual with his or her higher self and thus with the God-source. The word God in any language carries the highest vibrational frequency of any word in the language. Therefore, if one says audibly *I am God,* the sound vibrations literally align the energies of the body to a higher atunement.

Rick found no higher atunement through his mantra. He found only deepening problems. After realizing the danger, Rick finally told the counselors his mantra. They then bound it in the name of Jesus Christ and prayed for Rick to be able to forget it.

Today, Rick is free of the fear, the guilt, the drugs, the voices and the mantra. He is a new man, rejoicing daily in the victory Jesus gave him.

The dangers of contacting spirits are known even to secular ghost hunters. They warn that it is easy to get involved in the occult but horrifying and difficult to escape. Ed Warren, the director of the *New England Society for Psychic Research,* and his wife, Lorraine, have investigated more than 3,000 hauntings and demon possessions since 1946.

The Warrens found that many hauntings and possessions result from the use of Ouija boards, Tarot cards, seances and the like. Mrs. Warren has said that too many people dabble in the occult for kicks. "They try to conjure up spirits or ask questions they have no business getting involved in. What they don't realize is that the demon or bad spirit they invite in can follow them home and stay with them. That's when the *real* problems start."

It's easy to attract the attention of demons. Interest in the occult opens the door and announces to demons, "Here I am! I'm interested in what you can give me!" The more involved we get, the more we invite them in.

Some demons invite themselves into our lives in not-so-sneaky ways, albeit in disguise. The Unarius Academy of Sciences claims to consist of "countless thousands of Advanced Spiritual Beings." Prospective students are told that they'll be visited by space brothers. "Each and every student is helped from the inner and higher worlds, and from Uriel."

Uriel was Ruth Norman's spiritual name, supposedly given to her by the space brothers themselves. Saying it's an acronym for "Universal Radiant Infinite Eternal Light," she has claimed that Uriel is an archangel (although the Bible records no such angel name).

Isn't *that* a bit of self-glorification?

This New Age pusher made a frightening prediction: "In the not too distant future, the Unarius Science shall be taught in the public schools." By one name or another, it's already — though subtly — there.

As interest in the spirit world continues to increase, demons will increasingly take advantage of this opportunity. The number of haunted houses is climbing because interest in them is growing. A 1987 Epcot Center poll revealed that thirteen percent of Americans claim to have seen a ghost, one third said they believe in ghosts, and forty-two percent say they've contacted someone who's died. Among widows and widowers, almost two-thirds say they've contacted the dead.

Channeling owes its origins to *Spiritualism,* a major counter-religion based on necromancy — conjuring up spirits. (It is often called *spiritism* because it deals more with spirits than with spirituality.)

Modern-day Spiritism started when two attention-seeking teenagers, Margaret and Kate Fox, fooled the public into believing there were spirits in their house with whom they could communicate through a rapped-out code. The year was 1847; the place, Hydesville, New York. Although they admitted to fraud in 1886 and demonstrated they had made the rappings by cracking their toe joints, by then eleven million people had become too fascinated with the idea of spirit communication to believe their confession. To make Spiritism appear to be a legitimate religion, spiritists began to claim that their practices are compatible with Christianity.

Spiritism preaches what demons preach: there is no death and no judgment; Jesus was not the unique Son of God because we are all divine; Jesus was a martyr and a great medium, but He did not die to atone for our sins nor to conquer death because that was unnecessary.

The same themes come up in the theology of reincarnation, another occult belief popularized by channelers. People like to think they've led more exciting lives in the past. It's also a relief to believe that if we make mistakes, we'll have plenty of time to make up for them in future lives. Reincarnation is an attempt to escape God's wrath and final judgment without turning to Jesus Christ for our salvation.

Did you ever notice that many people who claim to remember past lives think they are reincarnations of famous people? Ruth Norman claimed to have been Socrates, Buddha, King Arthur, Peter the Great, and Mary Magdalene. She said her husband was Jesus of Nazareth — a denial of Christ's divinity and resurrection.

Emanuel Swedenborg said people become susceptible to false histories of past lives by believing in reincarnation.

He said these "recollections" are placed in people's minds by evil spirits. But believers in reincarnation don't want to even think about that. Many psychiatrists and psychologists who use hypnosis have been uncovering patients' "past lives." When they try to explain it, they call it a subconscious metaphor that symbolizes the patient's problem, or they say it's proof of reincarnation. They use "past life regression" as therapy because, they say, it works.

Normal psychotherapy failed Catherine* for eighteen months. She experienced anxiety, panic attacks and recurrent nightmares. She was terrified of the dark, of water and of being closed in. Without more information we can only guess that her problems might have indicated the interference of demons. That was never considered by her doctor.

During her second hypnosis session, the doctor told her to go back to the time her symptoms first began. Suddenly she was Aronda from 1863 B.C. Supposedly, Aronda had died from a flood. A week later, Catherine's fear of water disappeared. As she regressed to other "lives," she "recalled" other traumatic deaths, each related to current fears. Her symptoms improved dramatically.

Had demons been filling her with fear? Did demons take advantage of the hypnotic state to provide "memories" of past lives? Hypnosis can be dangerous because it opens our minds to other forces — including evil ones.

Garrett Oppenheim, a psychologist from Tappan, New York, has noticed that reincarnation therapy works best for people suffering from fears, anxiety attacks, depression and sometimes severe psychiatric illnesses — problems for which demons often are noted. He admitted it usually doesn't cure the illness, but the symptoms go away.

The fact that patients improve from past life regression keeps therapists returning to this method, which pleases

Satan to no end. Demons feed us stories of past lives because they want to lead us to ultimate destruction.

Read the words of a teenage girl who grew up with a strong relationship with Christ and yet, because she dabbled with the spirit world through seances, developed beliefs that pulled her farther and farther from God:

> "The Church teaches we should make the most of our lives for God while we are still alive, for when we die, our time is up. But I believe we continue working for God through eternity. When we die, we correct the wrong things we did when we were still alive by doing good things. Then, when we are reincarnated, we subconsciously try to lead a better life than the previous one, until we are so near perfect we reach the ultimate goal, unity with God.
>
> "The Bible says that God made man in His own image. Couldn't that really mean man was once a small part of God, and needs to progress spiritually to return to God?"

I wrote that in my diary one Sunday after church. This twisting of Bible verses is common among those involved in the occult. I was implying that man, being a small part of God, was once God Himself and can be again.

But this is impossible. We are *His* creation. When you build a bowl in ceramics class, it does not become you although it *can* represent you (your tastes, talent, style, etc.). Likewise, we are the earthen vessels God created and we are called to be representatives of His goodness and love. Being made in the image of God means we can reflect, like an image in a mirror, His tastes, talents, style, etc. It means our true nature is love, like His. But we are not God Himself. To think we are is idolatry.

Reincarnation is also popular because it relieves our sense of guilt about the countless victims of disease, abuse, poverty and early death. If we believe they are only suffering to correct the misdeeds of past lives, then we find no need to help relieve their misery. In fact, if we help them, we slow their progress toward perfection!

I shudder to think that this may account for the apathy so many people feel toward their fellow human beings. God wants to reach out His hand and heal the sick, rescue the abused, shower abundance on the poor, and restore life to those who have not yet lived a full life. The Bible confirms this in *Psalm* 72:12, 13 (NJB):

> *For he rescues anyone needy who calls to him,*
> *and the poor who has no one to help. He has pity*
> *on the weak and the needy, and saves the needy*
> *from death.*

He uses *us* to achieve this, not reincarnation. Because He gave us free will, we have to decide to rescue the needy. Most sickness and abuse and poverty and early death occur because we allow it. We fail to reach out to those in need. We fail to love. Apathy in the face of relievable suffering is one of the worst sins we commit.

Usually, we think it's beyond our power to love everyone enough to make a difference. That amount of love comes only from being in an active relationship with God, because He **is** love. The theory of reincarnation does not bring us to this realization.

Another fallacy of reincarnation is that when souls reach Nirvana, or oneness with God, they lose their sense of self, their individuality. This is not what God wants for us. After death, your personality will not die.

Look at the perfect example: When Jesus reached His perfection in the resurrection, He did not lose His individuality. His new, glorified body even retained the gruesome nail holes in his hands and feet. We, too, will receive immortal bodies—retaining our unique personalities—on the final Judgment Day if we follow God. *First Corinthians* 15:42-44 (NJB) tells us:

> *What is sown is perishable, but what is raised is imperishable; what is sown is contemptible but what is raised is glorious; what is sown is weak, but what is raised is powerful; what is sown is a natural body, and what is raised is a spiritual body.*

This glorious, powerful, immortal body is impossible to achieve without God's grace. *Hebrews* 9:27 (NAB) points out that reincarnation will not save us:

> *It is appointed that men die once, and after death be judged.*

So, too, we will not be saved by believing **we** are God. We need Jesus and His sacrifice (*Hebrews* 9:28 NAB):

> *Christ was offered up once to take away the sins of many; he will appear a second time . . . to bring salvation to those who eagerly await him.*

We can lose our salvation if we believe the voices of demons. As Pope John Paul II pointed out in his apostolic letter *Towards the Third Millennium:* "Christian revelation excludes reincarnation, and speaks of a fulfillment which man is called to achieve in the course of a single earthly existence." We find our identity only "through the sincere gift of self" (i.e., generously giving our time, our talents and our resources because we love others fully), "a gift which is made possible only through [our] encounter with God. . . this is the truth revealed by Christ."

---

* Not their real names.

---

[1] Cited by Jacques Vallee, *The Invisible College*, New York, NY: Dutton, 1975, p. 179.
[2] Abbot David Geraets, O.S.B., "Some Guidelines for the Spiritual Journey," *Catholic Charismatic*, Aug./Sept., 1979.

Chapter 7

Witchcraft: The Power of Magic

Witches wanted to bring darkness and ruin to the land. Using magic, they created a large, gloomy cloud.

This was a scene from a *"My Little Pony"* cartoon my children watched one morning when they were eight and six years old. The ponies, ever so clever, with the power of love and goodness on their side, defeated the witches by flying into the sky and blowing the cloud away.

"What's wrong with that story?" I asked David and Tammy.

"The ponies didn't ask God for help," David answered, remembering previous discussions.

"Right," I said. "But there's something more. Did you know there really are witches? And people sometimes do use magic to create clouds?"

I had once met a satanist who demonstrated the ability to form and then dissolve a cloud.

"Their magic comes from the devil, right?" David asked.

"Yes," I said. "But God can also create clouds. And He can make them disappear. Remember when we thought a tornado might be coming?"

I sure remembered. The conditions had been perfect for a tornado, and one had already touched down where the storm had been previously. I looked out of my living room and saw the trees bending violently, then looked at my children playing near me. I recalled how Jesus had calmed a storm in the gospel, so I reasoned that if I could do the same works Jesus did (as promised in *John* 14:12), I could calm *this* storm. With trust in God's protection, I commanded the storm, in Jesus' name and with the power of the Holy Spirit, to be still.

"As soon as I prayed for the wind to stop," I told my children, "it immediately turned into a gentle breeze."

I continued, "But when kids watch shows like this '*My Little Pony*' episode, they learn about magic but they don't learn that God is more powerful than witches. They don't hear that God tells us in the Bible never to use magic or sorcery. When kids who don't know God grow up and discover that there really are witches with magical powers, they often get interested in learning witchcraft. And they might never find out that God is better—unless we show them."

It's alarming how many cartoons and children's movies rely on magic for plot development. The youngsters who watch them are especially vulnerable to the allure of magic. It promises a sense of control in a world that seems so big, so scary, and ruled only by others. The magic becomes part of their fantasies. Even when the T.V. is off, the fantasy continues because they play with toy copies of the cartoon characters.

As children mature, fantasies evolve into dreams that become goals. Should we let society choose what our children fantasize? What goes into their imaginations will emerge in personality traits later.

That's why we should take a closer look at popular fantasy role-playing games such as *Dungeons and Dragons*. When Peter Leithart, a researcher for *American Vision*, of Atlanta, Georgia, and George Grant, author of several books on theology and social policy, studied these games, they concluded:

> Dungeons and Dragons is a dangerous game. It serves as an introduction to evil, a catechism of occultism, a primer for the ABCs of the New Age. It is a recruiting tool of Satan. It can alter the daily behavior of regular players. It stimulates the seamier side of our imaginations. It is an enormous-

ly attractive and effective escape for people frustrated with life. For many it becomes pure, obsessive fantasy, in its most destructive form.[1]

The game, created in 1973, is popular because of its mystical elements. How popular? Sales of *Dungeons and Dragons* nearly doubled every year since 1979. By 1985, it raked in over $100 million. Imitations of it have followed its lucrative path. By 1987, 250,000 to 300,000 fantasy role-playing games had sold, more than half of them to children. In 1980, forty-six percent were played by children ages ten to fourteen, another twenty-six percent by ages fifteen to seventeen.

The occult is a major element of the games. The most powerful players are those who use magic. The *Dungeon Master's Guide* teaches chanting, casting spells, communicating with spirits, and occultic symbols, many of them directly from witchcraft and satanism.

The games also involve sex, crime and violence. Is it good to fill imaginations with all this? It's been proven that the games often lead to obsessive escapism, schizophrenia, murders or suicides — definitely Satan's.

Dr. Gary North researched the games:

> Without any doubt in my mind, after years of study in the history of occultism, after having researched a book on the topic, and after having consulted with scholars in the field of historical research, I can say with confidence: these games are the most effective, most magnificently packaged, most profitably marketed, most thoroughly researched introduction to the occult in man's recorded history. Period.[2]

Michele Fritchie is one person who became its victim. After reading a newspaper article about *Dungeons and*

Dragons in 1978, she persuaded her mom to get it for her. She later told me, "I played the game and thought it was great. Though the rules stated it was a group participation game, nevertheless I played alone. For five years, I got more and more involved with it."

Although she had turned her life over to Jesus long before, the game began to rule her life. She couldn't wait to play with it. Even her family became uncomfortable with the time she spent engrossed in it.

In 1980, Michele found a game shop devoted to *Dungeons and Dragons* and began to add to her materials. She also subscribed to *Dragon* magazine and devoured every article, drawing and story. One article was even written by a Methodist minister who played the game and concluded there was nothing wrong with it!

When she heard warnings about the dangers of the game, she angrily defended it. Sure, it was violent and had evil characters, but it also had clerics and holy fighters, and good was supposed to triumph. "The fact is," she told me, "the game dealt with pagan gods and goddesses. And the game became a god to me. . . . I was held in bondage to that game for five years, during which I experienced depression, an evil temper, and even suicidal thoughts."

Fortunately, her interest in Christ remained intact enough for the Holy Spirit to reach her. She felt a desire to be filled with His presence and power. That inspired her to visit her favorite Christian bookstore. God's Spirit led her to a tract that condemned *Dungeons and Dragons*.

Something about that tract made her nervous. "I began to shake," she said. "I didn't know what was in that tract, but [it] hit a chord within me."

A few months later, the prayer group she belonged to addressed the problem of the occult. The dangers of the role-playing game came up again.

"That night, I couldn't sleep. God Himself caused me to wrestle with the issue. I slept only fitfully, tormented by the things God was throwing at me. Finally, at six in the morning, I yielded. Down came the game, the modules I'd spent at least $250 on, the issues of *Dragon* magazine with its artwork I had come to treasure—and I tore them up. I went to the kitchen, got some plastic trash bags and put it all in the garbage. Later, when the garbage men came, I watched them struggle with the somewhat overweight cans. I feared they would leave them, but take them they did. I was free at last."

Magic seduces the powerless. It appeals to those who feel victimized, those who seek to control circumstances or people. And don't we all feel powerless at times? When I was seventeen, I wanted to date a boy I'd met in Public Speaking class. Too shy to approach him, I waited for him to notice me.

A month passed and we still weren't saying more than hello, so I consulted a book on witchcraft for a spell to attract him. Little did I know that God already had plans for us to marry. I had prayed many times while growing up that the Lord would match me up with the right husband, and He had answered that prayer. But I was too impatient, too untrusting in the Lord to ask Him to arrange a date between me and Ralph.

Why does anybody need to resort to magic if our Father in Heaven loves us so much He really does want to grant us miracles and give us everything we need?

Using the definitions given by people in the occult, there are supposedly three kinds of magic (excluding prestidigitation, which is mere illusion): *neutral magic,* which uses a person's psychic abilities; *white magic,* which gets its power from "benign" spirits or gods for purposes such as protection, healing, luck, weather and fruitfulness; and *black magic,* which relies on evil spirits for purposes such as persecution, vengeance, destruction and death.

Does magic work? What is its source? Is white magic really better than black magic? Is neutral magic safe? Does using magic for good purposes justify its use?

Magic is the practice of manipulating psychic or supernatural power. It's different than relying on God's supernatural power, because magic is controlled by self regardless of God, while God's power is given to the extent and under the conditions that He knows is best, and we obtain it only through our relationship with Jesus and the Holy Spirit.

Magic comes in many forms, including witchcraft, voodoo, Satanism, sorcery, primitive religions, and even superstitions (including Christian superstitions, such as burying a statue of St. Joseph in order to sell a house — *praying* for the house to sell is not magic).

To witches, magic is a religious expression of psychic abilities. Ceremonial magic calls upon gods or spirits. Some say it relies on the powers of the unconscious mind. But what is its true source? What really makes it work?

Most witches insist their powers do not come from demons since they don't worship Satan. They worship the gods and goddesses of nature. But Paul told the Corinthians that worshiping anything but God is sacrificing to demons (1 *Cor.* 10:20 TLB):

> *What I am saying is that those who offer food to these idols are united together in sacrificing to demons, certainly not to God. And I don't want any of you to be partners with demons.*

The gods and goddesses of witchcraft are not impersonal forces. Witches know that these "deities" must be placated because allying with them can be dangerous — they can strike out and trap anyone whose rituals are not perfect. This is the opposite of Christianity. God does not strike out at anyone, including witches whose rituals are imperfect. Rituals do not release supernatural power as if they were magic formulas. Trust in a loving God and obedience to His Word — that is what releases the power of miracles.

Witches are partners with demons, whether they know it or not, whether they want to believe it or not. Since they do not worship Jesus Christ, their powers come from the only other supernatural source, which is Satan. Jesus said in *Matthew* 12:30 (NJB), "Anyone who is not with me is against me." Therefore, witches are anti-Christ. Witchcraft is satanic.

Witchcraft is a rebellion against God, a submission to Satan. If a magician uses the power of a demon, he becomes its slave. Sybil Leek, a famous contemporary American witch, boasted that witchcraft is a fulfilling religion *without* Jesus Christ or church—proof she has been a servant of the Enemy of Christ.

Magicians learn how to invoke unseen powers by studying the *grimoires*. These handbooks use the name of Moses to sound holy and are claimed to be lost books of the Old Testament. But this is deception. There are no such lost books in Jewish history. The grimoires are Satan's counterfeit of the Bible. Spells and incantations replace the promises of God.

Most witches claim to be free of Satan by using white magic. On the whole, they seem to be good people. They follow a common moral code: "Do what you want as long as it doesn't hurt anyone," not because they hear God calling them to holiness, but because they believe in the law of retribution: "Evil is repaid with evil, good deeds multiply the good done to you."

The aim of witchcraft is to make the person psychologically happier and more secure. This supposedly helps the magic work better because, they say, joyful people are in control of their lives and are thus better able to affect the world around them. Effective people work effective magic. Likewise, a strong will is necessary to employ the powers.

However, white magic is still magic: It relies on the powers of demons for personal, selfish purposes. "Do what you want as long as it doesn't hurt anyone" may be a good philosophy, but it's not Godly. It focuses on satisfying **our** desires without finding out what God wants us to do. As Dr. John Newport has said, "In essence [witchcraft] emphasizes ego-centricity or Satan-centricity instead of God-centricity."[3]

God tells us to honor Him above all things, to turn away from other gods. When we do, we open ourselves to receive whatever gifts He knows are best for us. We find out what those gifts are, and we grow to desire only these. Jesus promised this in *John* 15:7 (NJB):

> *If you remain in me and my words remain in you, you may ask for whatever you please and you will get it.*

Witchcraft beliefs and practices vary, but no witch truly knows God's love. If they did, they would immerse themselves in it. They would desire to do things His way because they would realize that His ways are really what's most fulfilling. Many witches are neopagans, a contemporary version of the ancient religion Wicca. Some are "natural" witches, relying on psychic abilities.

Feminist witches worship the ancient goddess of the moon, Diana. Some Dianic covens are explicitly lesbian, others are a mix of sexual preferences. A few include men. They reject the Judeo-Christian God because He is referred to in male terms.

Witchcraft is a pagan religion that worships the gods and goddesses of the ancient Celts, Teutons, Greeks or Egyptians. It goes back to one of the oldest religions of fertility, which is why witches venerate and worship nature and consider the highest deity to be female. Its roots also reach back to a stone-age cult honoring a horned god, who has become the goddess's mate.

Some witches honor a whole pantheon of gods, others one god and one goddess. The goddess, given different names by different covens, is a three-in-one deity of nature: earth goddess, moon goddess and fertility goddess.

Witches believe that humankind's salvation comes from a closer identification with nature, rather than from God the Son, Jesus. The rites and festivals (sabbats) of witchcraft tie in with the seasons, phases of the moon, equinoxes, solstices, and other natural rhythms.

New Year's Eve for witches is Halloween, also called *Samhain*. To them, it is the night of greatest power. So when we and our children dress up as witches on October 31 — or celebrate Halloween in any way, for that matter — we're actually honoring a sabbat of the witchcraft religion, even if we don't mean to.

The *sabbats*, open to prospective members, are times of worship, celebration and socializing. Whenever possible, they are held outdoors in a secret place. Witches use great care to ensure that no outsiders stumble upon them.

Esbats are closed meetings held weekly, at full and new moons, or whenever the coven chooses. Only members of the coven may participate. The ceremonies are extremely secretive, partly because they don't want to be discovered, and partly because they believe that secrecy aids magic.

Witches conjure up magical powers by summoning spirits or gods (demons), usually while staying inside a protective circle filled with a pentagram and other symbols. They call on the powers with ritual words, songs, meditation, sacred tools such as athames or wands, and sometimes sex. Nudity is often a part of it because they believe clothes block the flow of power.

Covens are important to witches because they believe working together increases magical powers. Usually, covens have thirteen members. Although modern witches frequently offer other reasons for this number, historically it has been a parody of Christ and His apostles.

Harmony among members is important in working the magic. Insincerity, animosity, or anything that causes nervous tension is said to reduce their powers.

To join a coven, a prospective member must take pre-initiation lessons. These vary, but often cover the range of occult practices. This includes the use of crystals, divination, astrology, astral projection, reincarnation (in witchcraft, there is no progression toward nirvana, but simply a returning to earth to live among loved ones), aura-reading, meditation, levitation and mind control. Divination ranges from Tarot cards, crystal balls and pendulums to interpreting dreams and contacting spirits in seances.

Prospects must clear their minds of Christian, Jewish and scientific beliefs and "misconceptions" about witchcraft. They're taught incantations, they learn to concentrate their mental energies and focus their wills, and they're shown how to draw energy into their souls for the ceremonies. They are told to open up to nature by talking to a tree and listening for its response.

During all this, the prospects have opened many doors to demonic influence. Unable to protect themselves because they don't have Christ, they have allowed demons to sink their claws deeper and deeper into their lives.

When the day comes for initiation, the ceremonies usually include a dedication, an oath of secrecy and final acceptance into the group. The new initiate begins to write her *Book of Shadows*, a record of the spells, rituals, songs and other things she learns, including her reflections about them. This is a sacred and personal book and must be destroyed upon the member's death.

Everything about witchcraft points to its demonic source: the name "Book of Shadows," secrecy, clearing the mind of beliefs about Christ, divination, the worship of gods and nature, the use of pentagrams, etc. White magic, neutral magic, black magic—God warns against it all. Even when it's used for good purposes, it comes from evil and ends with evil. It steals people away from God and His love and eternal joy in Heaven.

Isaiah tried to warn ancient Babylon about the dangers of turning to witchcraft instead of God, in *Isaiah* 47:9-11 (NJB):

> *Bereavement and widowhood will suddenly befall you in spite of your witchcraft and the potency of your spells. Confident in your wickedness, you thought, "No one can see me." Your wishes and your knowledge were what deluded you, as you thought to yourself, "I am the only one who matters." Hence, disaster will befall you which you will not know how to charm away, calamity overtake you which you will not be able to avert, ruination will suddenly befall you, such as you have never known.*

We simply cannot find true love, peace, and joy on this earth or in the afterlife if we manipulate the unseen world for magical powers. We can only receive that by trusting Jesus.

Christ's love is stronger than any magic. This was proven repeatedly when people first started spreading the good news of Christ's salvation. On one occasion, Philip arrived in a town that buzzed with excitement over the powers of a magician named Simon. When they heard Philip preach and saw the miracles he wrought, they were all converted. Even Simon recognized the greater power of Jesus Christ (*Acts* 8:9-25).

In another town where magic was practiced, many people had been contaminated and needed deliverance from demons (the magic arts books they later burned were worth fifty thousand silver pieces), so many that Paul couldn't get to them all. He had to hand out blessed handkerchiefs to heal them (*Acts* 19:11-20).

Elsewhere, Paul and Barnabas overpowered a magician named Bar-Jesus, who tried to keep an important leader from learning about Christ. This story is told in *Acts* 13:9-11 (NJB):

> *Then . . . Paul, filled with the Holy Spirit,*
> *looked at him intently and said, "You utter*
> *fraud, you imposter, you son of the devil, you*
> *enemy of all uprightness, will you not stop*
> *twisting the straightforward ways of the Lord?*
> *Now watch how the hand of the Lord will strike*
> *you: you will be blind, and for a time you will*
> *not see the sun." That instant, everything went*
> *misty and dark for him, and he groped about to*
> *find someone to lead him by the hand.*

What leads a person into witchcraft? Because of the secrecy surrounding covens, it's impossible to know how many people become witches. However, a 1980 estimate said there were at least twenty thousand, perhaps as many as a hundred thousand, worldwide. Certainly the lure of magic, the excitement of secrecy, and the fun of doing something forbidden all contribute.

Witchcraft attracts people for the same reasons as other occult practices. It's a search for supernatural power, usually because they are dissatisfied with their lives due to the feeling that they aren't experiencing enough love. Witches want the power and love of God in their lives, but they don't know there is a God who wants to give it to them. They've been deceived into thinking that there is no loving, powerful Father in Heaven, that they cannot trust Christ. The only way for them to find out what God is really like is if Christians love them unconditionally and serve them generously, doing good to them so that they are exposed to God's true nature.

Most witches practice white magic, i.e., they want to use good supernatural powers, but they don't realize they are tapping into evil powers. They don't realize it is really God for Whom they are searching and that He offers the greatest supernatural power of all. They don't see any advantage to turning away from witchcraft and other areas of the occult.

For Claire*, the road to witchcraft started early in her upbringing. She was raised in a Christian family and taken to church, but her religious experience was more confusing than satisfying. Her mother was Catholic but insisted the children go to their father's Protestant church. Didn't Mom find her original faith meaningful? If not, why didn't she convert? Claire wanted to know. Her dad didn't go to church at all, yet he believed in God. Did her parents really believe church was important?

These inconsistencies in her parents' attitudes about religion made going to church seem unimportant. In Sunday school, Claire had learned about Jesus, but she never learned why—or how—to have a relationship with Him. She felt closer to God sitting in her secret place by a pond in the woods.

Since her father seemed to have the most faith in the family, and he rarely went to church, Claire decided that she, too, could believe in God without going to church. Parents, especially fathers, need to realize how important their example is. Studies reveal that if both parents attend church regularly, seventy-nine percent of their children remain faithful to their upbringing. If only the dad goes, fifty percent of the children stay in the Church. If only the mother goes, the number drops all the way down to *fifteen* percent. And if the children are sent to religious education classes and/or church, but neither parent attends worship services, only *six* percent believe religion is important.

Claire searched for God, but she thought she could only find Him at the pond. There she learned to pray, although she didn't know it was prayer. She talked to God and she talked to nature, not sure if there was a difference between the two, hoping someone or Someone was listening. She asked questions about her life that were to go unanswered for years: Who was God? What did He have to do with her? Why did people *want* to go to church? What was she missing?

The supernatural began to intrigue her when she received a Ouija board for Christmas. It was just a game to her, and when the novelty wore off, the board got buried in the closet.

During her teenage years, she played at having seances with friends, pretending to see and hear ghosts. Then her older sister, Suzette*, bought a new deck of Tarot cards and gave the old set to Claire. Sometimes Claire would lay out the cards and the readings would be very accurate. There was something beyond the norm here, but she refused to let the cards determine her life.

Suzette became interested in astrology and learned to write horoscopes. Claire let her draw them up for her, but she decided they were only as true as a person reads into them.

Suzette started experimenting with astral projection, auras, levitation and numerology. She taught some of it to her little sister. That was when Claire discovered that Suzette had joined a witches' coven.

Witchcraft seemed fun, too. Claire's earlier prayers to nature by the pond made witchcraft especially appealing. Plus it was mystical, magical, and something to do behind mom and dad's back. By now, Claire was sixteen and already rebelling. She asked Suzette to teach her more.

The two believed that their occult studies led them closer to truth. Suzette became a high priestess. Then, when the coven bought a house to form a commune, Claire visited her in the new place. The exposure to the other witches increased her curiosity. Discovering the unknown was fascinating, dabbling in magic exciting. But, just to be safe, she decided she would not commit herself entirely to it.

Still, the coven appealed to her. This was a group of people who belonged to each other. Claire, tired of being an outsider, asked to join. Before she could be initiated, the coven had to vote on her. Suzette being of high rank gave Claire an edge, but the group had to go through the usual procedures.

Claire was brought before the coven in their ceremony room. The members sat in a circle in white robes with pentagram necklaces. Claire sat in the middle while they asked her questions: "What do you know about witch-craft? What do you think a coven is? Do you know our sabbats?"

They drilled her on witchcraft knowledge. Then they asked: "Would you do something illegal because the group did it?"

Claire answered, "That would depend on what it was and why."

"Would you harm someone because the group was doing it?"

"No. If I think something's wrong, I won't do it."

"Would you do something if Suzette did it or told you to do it?"

"No."

When the questioning ended, they asked her to wait in the kitchen. They had been impressed by her strong will, her determination and knowledge. They invited her to join the circle. Then they "passed the power." Holding hands and chanting, they concentrated on sending energy from one person to the next. Claire felt it go through her.

To prepare Claire for initiation, they set up study groups for six nights. She would be instructed in the various forms of supernatural power by different members of the coven. On the first night, they taught Claire astral projection and thought power, starting with how to concentrate on people to get them to move their arm.

Claire noticed that her presence added something unexpected to the group. Whenever she was with them, the other members squabbled with each other. They didn't fight other times, Suzette told her. Claire wondered if she was, somehow, an unnerving influence. Perhaps it was the doubts, the skepticism she still carried. Or perhaps it was her unwillingness to submit totally. She knew that the members practiced telepathy and she could sense when someone tried to probe her thoughts. She frustrated them by building a mental wall, brick by brick, between her and the intruder.

Perhaps Claire brought with her a power greater than theirs, because she actually still believed in God instead of the god and goddess the coven worshiped. Claire never made it to the second study group meeting. The coven had disbanded.

Several years later, Claire finally found the answers to her childhood questions. She learned that God is the Creator of all and that He cared about her. She discovered the power of having a relationship with Jesus Christ. She realized people want to go to church because it's a place to experience God and grow closer to Him.

At last she knew what had been missing for so long: a personal relationship with Jesus Christ.

---

* Not their real names

---

[1] Peter Leithart and George Grant, *A Christian Response to Dungeons and Dragons*, Fort Worth, TX: Dominion Press, 1988, p.16.

[2] Cited by Leithart and Grant, *A Christian Response to Dungeons and Dragons*, p.9.

[3] Dr. John Newport, *The Biblical and Occult Worlds — A 20th Century Confrontation* tape series, Fort Worth, TX: Latimer House Publishing Co., 1973, "The Christian and Magic."

Chapter 8

Satanism: The Power of Horror

Warning: Satanism is the ugliest, most gruesome side of the occult. It includes bizarre, evil deeds that go beyond the normal imagination, deeds you would think are beyond the capacity of human beings. Anything horrible that demons can figure out to do, this is what they manipulate their followers into doing. Therefore, you might not want to read this chapter, so if you don't have an absolutely necessary reason to learn about Satanism, skip ahead to the next chapter.

There is much of its gruesomeness that I leave out simply because we should protect our minds from such horrors. However, I do try to portray Satanism accurately. The purpose of this chapter is not to terrify you but to bring Christ's victory to those readers who have any interest at all in Satanism, or might now or in the future know someone who does. It is also intended to demonstrate the need for all Christians to respond — with Christ. None of us can ignore this trend any more.

Satanism has penetrated nearly every community. Interest in it has been fueled by heavy metal music with satanic overtones, by world problems that seem out of control, by public acceptance of the New Age, and by Halloween, which is Satan's high holy day.

Satanism is much more active in America than the media portray. Satanists are extremely secretive. Most of the murders, sexual abuse and other crimes committed as satanic rituals go unpublicized.

Ted Gunderson, a cult investigator for the FBI, reported, "There is a network of [satanists] across the country who are very active. They have their own rest and relaxation farm. They are in contact with each other. . . . They have their own people who specialize in surveillances and photography and in assassinations."

Dr. Wayne A. VanKampen of the *Bethesda Psychiatric Institute* in Denver, Colorado, the first hospital in America to establish a department for treating the victims of satanic crimes, recently said, "I believe involvement in Satanism is increasing . . . and I believe it demands our attention."

When the media cover violent crimes, they often miss the connection to Satanism. When the connection is obvious, the media tend to sensationalize it. The reaction by authorities then is usually to prevent public hysteria by downplaying Satanism's presence. But very often, where there is a macabre crime, there is also Satanism.

On November 1 (the day after Halloween), 1987, six-year-old Lisa Steinberg became a national symbol of child abuse when Joel Steinberg, her father by illegal adoption, fatally beat her. In the great amount of publicity her case received, little was mentioned of the satanic cult to which her parents belonged, even though the defense attorney for Joel Steinberg stated that influence.

Neither was there much said about little Lisa being taken to the cult's ceremonies. But she had drawn pictures of it. In one, she depicted herself wearing a robe decorated with a pentagram and a descending crescent moon—satanic symbols. She had worn that costume during rituals and she had said that it frightened her.

Wouldn't knowing that Satanism does result in abuse and sometimes murder help law enforcers and family members prevent some crimes? Thomas Wedge, a former Union, Ohio, deputy sheriff and author of *The Satan Hunter*, has told law enforcement groups that satanists thrive on police ignorance and disbelief.

In fact, don't we all thrive on ignorance and disbelief about Satanism? We can't bear to think that it's a big problem, because we feel powerless to do anything about it, forgetting that God working through us can accomplish whatever is needed. If the parents of a Jefferson Township, New Jersey, boy had known the warning signs and dangers, perhaps a tragedy would have been averted. (For a list of warning signs, see Appendix B.)

Fourteen-year-old Tommy Sullivan was raised in a moral, middle-class home and attended Catholic school. He became interested in Satanism when a classmate wrote a report about it for religion class.

One has to wonder why the teacher accepted this report, or why school officials didn't use it as an opportunity to teach about the dangers of Satanism, or why the school's principal didn't explain Christ's victory over Satan.

In just two short months, Tommy was deep enough into Satanism to brutally kill his mother with a Boy Scout knife and then commit suicide.

The manner of his death reveals beyond any doubts that demons were active: Tommy slashed both wrists deep enough to sever the tendons and snap the hands back. Despite his now-useless hands and the rapid loss of blood, he was still able to slit his throat from ear to ear all the way to the spinal column, nearly taking off his own head.

There had been warning signs. He loved heavy metal music with its satanic messages. Heavy metal posters and satanic symbols filled his bedroom. His teachers and parents watched his personality change drastically. His drawings screamed of his fascination with Satan, including one which ominously depicted a man in a devil's costume ready to plunge a knife into a woman. Even his friends became afraid of him.

He had signed a contract with the devil, part of which read: "I believe that evil will once again rise and conquer the love of God." He also wrote that he'd kill his parents and himself in order to "go directly to hell to work with [Satan] as a demon."

There are two forms of Satanism: in one, members are recruited into it; in the other, members are born into it (generational Satanism).

Ninety percent of recruited satanists are teenagers. They are usually white males between the ages of fourteen and twenty with above-average intelligence. What sets them on the road to Satan? Experts have found a common thread among teenage satanists. Most have already gotten into drugs and alcohol. The vast majority of them are obsessed with heavy metal music. Most have low self-esteem and many are suicidal.

Kevin Murphy, an officer with the Yonkers, New York, Police Department who teaches police and health professionals about Satanism, has remarked, "[Satanism] worries me more than other kinds of teen rebellion because the profile for a suicidal kid is so similar to a cult-related kid."

Satanism offers troubled teens a sense of power. Usually, they feel socially isolated and misunderstood by family and classmates. They've experimented with drugs and do poorly in school. They already see themselves as "weird,"so they're looking for acceptance where weird is good. Inside, they're living with deep-seated rage. Many are angry at God. Mounting frustrations give way to fantasy and thoughts of revenge. Satanism is a way to rebel. It seems to justify deviant behavior and offer approval of their feelings, but in turn it increases their violence and isolation from normal society.

Satanists are looking for ways to improve bad situations. They are searching for answers, even a reason for being, but when their life situations get worse — as they do when caught in Satan's trap — they plunge in even deeper, and become desperately willing to try even more.

Initially, many follow their friends into it, not realizing they're actually worshiping Satan. Some start with drugs and get so high, they are easily led into doing what they normally would not do.

At parties, satanists observe non-members to find good candidates for recruitment. Then they invite them to experiment with the occult, sometimes using role-playing games such as *Dungeons and Dragons*. If the candidates show interest, the satanists teach them various occult powers, whetting their appetites, getting them hooked on the drug of playing with the devil.

Unlike their adult counterparts, teenage satanists are less interested in devil worship as a religion than as a form of rebellion. They are generally satisfied with hanging the neighborhood cat or some other easy-to-catch animal, chanting around a bonfire, getting high, drawing graffiti, and performing other anti-society acts. They don't feel a need for the ceremonies of organized cults. They're more interested in the shock value of Satanism. It's a cry for attention. It's a scream of pain from deep-seated problems with which the teenager can no longer cope. It's a plea for help.

They don't really understand what they're really getting into. They don't know the power of Satan or the desire he has to keep them from God. They don't realize that they are inviting demons to make their trouble-filled lives even worse. Tommy Sullivan surely didn't want to kill his mother and himself when he started exploring Satanism.

When teens fool with Satan, it should not be perceived as a passing phase, as many parents have done. The demons make sure the interest will not pass. The only way out is intervention by breaking Satan's hold through the power of Jesus.

Pete Roland's mother learned this too late. Pete and three other teenagers clubbed a friend to death with baseball bats in Carl Junction, Missouri. After he was arrested, his mother, Penny Baert, realized she had seen the warnings.

"Pete gradually withdrew from family life," she said. "He even got to where he avoided any meals with us. He listened to the heavy metal music at every opportunity. I saw the album covers and they're hideous. I just assumed that if they sell it, it's got to be okay. I saw satanic symbols on his bookwork and I spoke to him about it. Didn't mean anything. I assumed it was a passing phase."

Pete ended up doing something he never would have done without Satan's influence. "It basically started out with the killing of animals," he said from a maximum-security prison in Fulton, Missouri. "Sometimes I thought I wasn't the master of my own body, like something else kind of took over."

After ending up in prison, Pete Roland discovered that Satan's promises of power and fulfillment were lies. "I felt real empty inside," he said. "I could never love again. Like a zombie."

Sean Sellers, a young man sentenced to death for killing his mother, stepfather and a convenience store clerk, said, "The murders were a sacrifice to prove allegiance to Satan, to prove my hatred towards society and everything."

After Sellers realized Satan had betrayed him by letting him get caught, he wanted to quit. He discovered, "There is no way out of Satanism except through Jesus Christ."

Most devil worshipers trust Satan because they're led to believe that he has more to offer than God.

"He's someone who loves me, someone who cares about what happens to me. He is not evil," said Debbie, a twenty-six-year-old satanist from a quiet suburban town on the East Coast. At the time, she'd been a satanist for little more than a year.

She had started with witchcraft, but after three years she craved more power. She tried asking God for things and when the answers she wanted didn't come, she decided He didn't care about her.

Where were the Christians who could have pointed her to a true relationship with Christ, the kind of relationship that would have given Debbie the help she sought?

She'd been looking for a god she could manipulate, but she needed the God Who didn't need to be manipulated because He already truly loved her. Where were the Christians who could have revealed His love to her by giving her genuine help and unconditional caring?

Finding no such help, Debbie turned to Satan. She bought *The Satanic Bible* and learned how to dedicate herself to God's enemy. Demons jumped at the opportunity. Immediately, things began to change in her life—changes Debbie enjoyed.

A car accident had previously left her with no feeling from the waist down. After becoming a satanist, almost all sensation returned. Through spells and rituals, she began to get money and anything else she wanted. When someone wronged her, she called on demons to right it. She told them the problem and the demons took it from there. When the other person then experienced misfortune, Debbie felt no guilt about it because, she believed, "It was the demons who did it, not me!"

"I believe Satan loves us more [than God does]," she said. "If God really loved His children, he wouldn't let half of what happens to kids happen. He wouldn't let His kids get beat up. Satan protects me. He takes care of me."

For now.

Debbie was never introduced to the love of God. Abused as a child, she never learned from her parents that God loved her or could help her. She grew up with low self-esteem; Satanism gave her a way to believe in herself. She found that Satan "allowed" her to use power she already had within her. "Now I know I can conquer anything," she said.

Like many recruited satanists, Debbie believed a favorite deception: Satan is Lucifer, son of God, and he rules the earth while God rules the heavens.

This is a typical half-truth. God did create Satan, so in that sense he's God's son. But Satan severed his ties with God, so he's a son no more. And Satan does rule the earth, but God is the highest authority on earth *and* in the heavens, and anyone who follows Jesus also has authority over Satan.

Debbie was told that Satan was her creator: "He made me. He is not evil. The churches [say he's evil] because they need him to survive." This is the excuse many satanists use to justify their worship of the devil.

Another of Debbie's beliefs is common to both forms of Satanism (the recruited and the generational): "The day is going to come when Satan's going to come. He's going to appear. On that day, people will have to choose."

It's true. The Bible says the Anti-Christ will appear. People will have to choose between Christ and Satan. Then Christ will rid the world of Satan and all his demons and disciples, and give glorious, everlasting, sin-free life to everyone who chooses to be on God's side (see *Rev.* chapters 20, 21). Satan lies about who will be the victor.

Although Debbie believed Satan loves her, he's not been nice to her. From the start, he's given her a foreshadowing of what was in store for her if she died as his follower. Whenever she asked demons to do something for her, she'd be nearly destroyed in fires. She reasoned that Satan was letting her know that she had to pay for what she wanted. Indeed, Satan always exacts a price from his worshipers — but a price far higher than they know.

How different her life would have turned out if the Christians around her — friends, teachers, neighbors, and church members who came knocking to distribute pamphlets — had gotten involved, identified her needs, showed that they cared, and gave her unconditional love and attention no matter how she behaved.

Once people get involved with Satan, at first they willingly continue because Satan promises to give them whatever they ask. Of course, the "good" he does only leads to disaster. Soon he controls them, and he won't ever let go unless a stronger power makes him let go. The only stronger power is Jesus Christ.

If satanists decide to quit on their own, their superiors usually threaten to torture them or kill their families. In hard-core cults and generational covens, members who want to leave are sometimes punished by being hung upside down in a pit filled with animal parts, blood, rats, snakes and spiders. In severe cases, it might even include the body parts and blood of other disobedient cult members. They are frightened into feeling completely trapped.

The longer satanists remain, the more Satan restructures their minds. At first they go from evil to evil to gratify every desire and to gain more power. Then they become so egotistical and arrogant, they think they are above the law. Some go even further and become psychopaths or sociopaths, unable to recognize right from wrong. They want to prove they can get away with whatever crime they choose.

Many serial killers, including David Berkowitz (Son of Sam), Ted Bundy, Henry Lee Lucas, and Richard Ramirez (the Night Stalker) were devil-worshippers. Charles Manson has often described himself as the incarnation of the devil and has been revered by many satanists.

One Manson fan, Nikolas Schreck, has said, "We would like to see most of the human race killed off because it is unworthy of the gift of life. A blood bath would be a cleansing and a purification of a planet that has been dirtied and degraded for too long." If only he knew that Christ already shed His blood for this purpose, that through Him we can all be cleansed of our sins and create a better world!

Generational satanists are better at hiding their psychopathological attitudes and behaviors. Steven* was one of those who are born into it. He was dedicated to the devil by his parents in a secret ceremony that mocked Christian baptism. Actually, he never knew who his real parents were. Many female cult members are raped in ceremonies and become breeders for sacrifices. Their pregnancies and babies are hidden from the public so there is no proof they ever existed. When demons require more than the sacrifice of an animal, children are occasionally used because of their innocence.

Steven might have been sacrificed, except the coven members determined he had the potential to become a high priest. They decided this by consulting demons and astrological charts, and by observing him for psychic abilities and compliancy. Compliancy was essential, because if he had a strong will, he would be hard to control.

While still an infant, he was "rebirthed" to the wife of the high priest. As the years passed, he was taught to follow in his father's footsteps. When he resisted, he was tortured psychologically, and sometimes physically.

He learned how to act in public like a normal person who didn't know a thing about Satanism. He went to church with his family—a Christian church of a mainstream, non-conservative denomination. He even attended Sunday School, and no one outside of his coven had the slightest idea that anything was wrong.

One night, while still very young, Steven was told it was time to start performing his own sacrifices. He did not want to do it. However, his high priest father convinced him that if he didn't comply, *he* would become the sacrifice. It might have been a lie, but little Steven was too terrified to suspect that. He wanted out of this horrible trap!

His father placed him on the altar. Then Steven remembered that the Sunday School teacher had said that Jesus loved him.

"Jesus!" he called out. "Jesus, help me!"

Suddenly, a bright light came from nowhere and surrounded him. The other satanists were stunned and confused; they couldn't bear to be near this light. They fled in panic. Steven was left alone with Jesus.

He never forgot the experience, although his father later punished him for it. The coven spent time manipulating his mind so that he came to believe that Jesus really hated him.

After he grew up and became the high priest he was supposed to be, he entered a well-known theological seminary of a non-conservative denomination. Like many other satanists, his goal was to help Satan infiltrate the Christian Church to destroy it from within. However, Jesus arranged for him to meet someone who had escaped from Satanism. She recognized his need to get counseling for his addictions and low self-esteem, two of the results of Satan worship that he had not been able to hide. She sent him to a Christian therapist.

While undergoing therapy, he turned his life over to Jesus Christ. Once more, Jesus came powerfully to surround him and love him and help him. When his old coven found out, they tried to kidnap him or kill him, but each time, Jesus protected him supernaturally.

Steven began a long process of emotional recovery. It will take a lifetime for him to fully heal, but he is living a normal, healthy, Christ-centered life. He graduated from the seminary, switched denominations, was ordained a Baptist minister, and opened a Christian counseling agency to help others escape from the addictions and psychological wounds of the occult.

Someone must have been praying for Steven. It takes the intervention of Christians who care to help people get out of Satanism, but it's not easy. The occult can be more addictive than drugs and alcohol. Satan worship becomes a trap from which there seems to be no escape. Therapists who don't ask Jesus to drive away demons fail to get rid of the demonic influence. When teenagers are recruited into Satanism, their parents often drive them deeper into it by opposing them.

If you're such a parent, what your child needs is love,

patience, and spiritual warfare (see chapters ten and eleven). Intervening when—or before—a child first shows interest in Satanism is the best strategy. But whenever you get involved, sit down with the child, listen to his problems, help him find solutions and healing, work at raising his self-esteem, and pray. Rely on the victory Jesus already won over the demons.

Likewise, if you know someone who's been a victim of ritual abuse, they won't really be free of the torture or have peace until they've experienced the healing of Christ. Unfortunately, churches and pastors are often unprepared to deal with this problem. According to Lauren Stratford, author of *Satan's Underground* and childhood victim of ritualistic sexual abuse and pornographic exploitation, "One of the major hurdles victims of Satanism face is finding a church that will accept them" and help them.

Christians have a very powerful weapon against Satanism, the love of Jesus Christ. We give them that love by praying for them and by continually doing good to them, loving them unconditionally, and showing that we care—over and over again so that they finally begin to believe it.

Although Satanism's popularity has exploded only lately, it has existed since humans first chose to worship gods who were not God. By the seventh century of Christianity, distorted versions of the Mass were used to work magic. In the fourteenth century, people used Black Masses as a protest. In the sixteenth century, European aristocrats worshiped Satan.

For the most part, Satan worship was forced underground until an Englishman, Aleister Crowley, revived it in the early part of this century. Crowley, who described himself as the most evil man in the world, had been a disciple of Theosophy founder Madame Blavatsky.

In 1966, self-avowed sorcerer Anton LaVey created the *Church of Satan* in California. He later served as a consultant for the movie *Rosemary's Baby* and played the part of the devil in it. He helped with other occult movies, too.

When he used the church for his personal glory and financial income, his senior initiate, Michael Aquino, rebelled. Aquino formed the *Temple of Set* by invoking the Prince of Darkness. That was 1975. Since then, the Temple has been building a nationwide network of satanic covens, bookstores, and New Age centers that anyone with a computer modem can access through the Temple's location on the Internet.

Satanic organizations have been wielding their power against all of us. According to Dianne Core, the head of England's *Childwatch* organization, which investigates child abuse, satanists from all over the world have gathered to plan strategies. She told the International Martin Luther King Tribunal in Rome, Italy, "The decision was made to create a spiritual desert in our lives today, to infiltrate all aspects of family life and society, so that the morality that bound us together would be undermined and that the young would be rendered defenseless against the forces of evil."

In 1969, LaVey published *The Satanic Bible*, which quickly became very popular and has remained so. Preaching that people should do anything they want to do as long as it's not against the law, this best-seller has become the handbook for anyone interested in rebelling against Christianity and society through the occult, and anyone looking for supernatural power from the devil.

Typical of the evil this book teaches is how to cast curses. It says, "If your curse provokes their actual annihilation, rejoice that you have been instrumental in ridding the world of a pest."

Most buyers of this book are teenagers. Many of them have already been desensitized to evil by watching horror films. The majority of horror movie audiences are teenagers, and they are no longer appalled at the violence they see there. They laugh at it and yell for the bad guys to get their next victims. They've become excited by the power of evil, so they turn to *The Satanic Bible* for an even greater thrill—the thrill of bringing supernatural power from the screen into their lives.

Micki* bought the book at age seventeen because she'd been interested in the supernatural since she was a little girl. Her parents had taken her to horror movies and she had always enjoyed horror stories, Dracula, and books about the occult.

When she read *The Satanic Bible*, her interest became an obsession. Soon she was practicing witchcraft. She put hexes on people with whom she'd fought and concocted love spells for friends. Schoolmates began coming to her for occult advice.

A satanist learned of her reputation and approached her. He was the twenty-five-year-old leader of a satanic coven. He invited her to join his group. Micki saw this as an opportunity for greater power, so she eagerly agreed. But before she was allowed in, she had to pass an interview and then get initiated.

During the interview, the leader asked:

"Have you ever done anything illegal?"

"Have you ever taken drugs? What kind? How often?"

"How would you feel about sacrificing animals?"

"Are you a virgin? How many men have you had sex with? Have you had sex with women or children?"

Apparently, she gave him the answers he wanted. He told her that initiation into the coven would mean having sex with both male and female cult members. Then they would take drugs and perform the necessary ceremonies.

However, Micki could not bring herself to do the required sex acts. She lost her chance to join.

That pull of her conscience was a turning point. It gave Jesus a chance to reach her. Since then, she has rejected the occult and become a Christian. When she looked back on her interest in Satan, she blamed the books she read for playing a large part.

"The more evil you read, the more evil you become,"

she said. "You start feeling like you have power. If you keep reading more, you will get power. . . . You get so absorbed, you want to try everything."

Satanism is the direct opposite of Christianity. Its members are taught that good is evil and evil is good, that Satan is the rightful Prince of Heaven and that Jesus is the liar, that God cheated Satan by casting him out of Heaven to make room for Jesus, and that Satan is gathering an army that will someday conquer God's Kingdom.

Black Masses are mockeries of the Holy Communion of Christ. Occult experts Clifford Wilson and John Weldon describe a Black Mass in their book, *Occult Shock and Psychic Forces:*

> Normally, a small group of people sit in front of a table covered with a purple velvet altar cloth, lit with candles. Over the "altar" hangs a cross upside down and a picture of the devil, half-human, half-beast. A high priest stands by the table dressed in bishop's robes. On his person he wears an inverted cross. He throws a larger cross to the floor. . . . He then spits upon the cross, with an obscene gesture, and cries, "Hail Satan!" Thus begins the sickening and blasphemous ritual, as the devil worshippers repeat the Lord's prayer backwards and make mockery of the ordinances of the church.[1]

Specific rituals vary from coven to coven. Most teenager satanists invent their own ceremonies. Hard core practitioners steal body parts from cemeteries and religious artifacts from Catholic and Episcopal churches for use in ceremonies. Communion Hosts (bread that is consecrated and becomes the body of Jesus) are desecrated and eaten, and they mix blood and urine with the wine they drink.

The Bible warns about this in *Hebrews* 10:29 (NJB):

> *And you may be sure that anyone who tramples on the Son of God, and who treats the blood of the covenant which sanctified him as if it were not holy, and who insults the Spirit of grace will be condemned to a far severer punishmen'*

Heavy metal music plays a large part. While not all heavy metal is satanic, some of it has artwork and lyrics that glorify Satan. So do the stage antics of their performers. Almost every teenager who has committed a violent act in the name of Satan has been obsessed with the music.

Since the 1960s, music has been used to promote increasingly harmful ideas. According to Dr. T.L. Tashjian, chairman of psychiatry at Philadelphia's Mount Sinai Hospital, rock music has significantly affected the formation of values among children. The trend toward darker, more dangerous lyrics is culminating today in heavy metal music. Dr. William C. Scott, chairman of the *American Medical Association*, Council on Scientific Affairs, has said that this presents "a real threat to the physical health and emotional well-being of especially vulnerable children and adolescents."

What proof do we have that the music is harmful? Look at the statistics. In 1990, the juvenile violent crime arrest rate climbed to 430.6 per 100,000, which is up from 137 per 100,000 in 1965. Murders committed during the 1980s by kids ages ten through seventeen soared nearly ninety percent.

Consider this: Ninety percent of youths arrested for bias-related or occultic crimes are involved with heavy metal music, particularly the "black metal" bands.

Although metal rock fans often say they listen to the music for its sound and not the lyrics, a study revealed that ninety percent of them admit to knowing the words, and sixty percent agree with the message of the words.

This is alarming, because many of the songs focus on doom and gloom, death and suicide, blood and violence. The lyrics often contain satanic rituals and actual oaths to Satan. Many others carry implied messages that promote immorality.

Some lyrics are outright satanic. Some, though not mentioning Satan, promote sado-masochism, murder, suicide, sexual deviance, hatred, bigotry, violence, and occult practices. Still others promote drug and alcohol abuse, prostitution, profanity, homosexuality, promiscuity, rebellion, and other immoral behaviors that have been expressed through music for decades.

The music has inspired teenagers to cut their arms and share in the drinking of each other's blood. According to Pete Roland, "After you listen to this [music] three or four hours a day every day for years or months, it can get to you."

It's dangerous to expose ourselves to anything that glorifies horror, whether it's in music, movies or books. God tells us through Paul in *Philippians* 4:8 (RSV):

> *Finally, brethren, whatever is true, whatever is honorable, whatever is just, whatever is pure, whatever is lovely, whatever is gracious, if there is any excellence, if there is anything worthy of praise, think about these things.*

Focusing our attention on good things brings us closer to God, closer to His love, and closer to the wealth of supernatural gifts God wants to give us. Focusing on evil and horror, though the heavy metal musicians deny this, lures us into a fascination with the devil, leads us away from a moral, God-centered life, and dumps us into a life of destruction.

Destruction is the trademark of the devil. Satanic rituals are bizarre at best, unbelievably grotesque at their worst. They seem too horrible to be true, but the stories given by survivors are too consistent, too much alike not to be taken seriously.

However—and this is extremely important—we should not be afraid of Satan. Once fear sets in, we, too, are his victims. If we think every case of child abuse is due to a satanic cult, if we think Satan's influence on people always means they're possessed by demons, or if we attribute everything that goes wrong in our lives to Satan's interference, then we are his victims.

A case in point is the story of a sixteen-year-old girl, Beth*, who had twice tried to commit suicide. Her mother took her to prayer meetings to expel the spirit of suicide, but it didn't work. Even though lots of people were praying for her, Beth tried to kill herself again. Finally, the mother went to a Irene Huber at the Marian Center and said, "You've got to lay hands on my daughter and expel the demon!"

Irene sat her down to find out more. "When was the last time your daughter had a complete physical examination?" she asked.

"Oh, not for several years."

"Before I pray for her, take her to a good doctor. Then come back and tell me what the results are."

The doctor discovered that the girl had severe diabetes. With an altered diet and medication, her system stabilized and her suicidal tendencies disappeared.

The mother had blamed Satan for Beth's problems. In so doing, she gave Satan the opportunity to make things worse. He was happy she blamed him instead of going to a doctor. The delay gave the daughter more time to kill herself.

Of course, had this girl been involved in the occult, prayers to expel demonic influences most certainly would have been necessary to supplement the medicine. One cannot use the devil without being enslaved by him. However, we must seek healing from all sources that God gives us, including doctors, counselors and prayer warriors.

One final, important note: We should not think of ourselves as superior to those who get sucked into Satan worship. Each of us is guilty of doing some things that Satan inspires. What activities do we get into that God wants us to avoid? What in our lives do we put ahead of God? When have we failed to love others unconditionally, refusing or neglecting to serve them generously? This is how we honor the devil. This is why we all need the victory of Jesus Christ—every day.

To conquer Satan, we need to rely on the words of 1 *John* 3:8 (NJB):

> *This was the purpose of the appearing of the Son*
> *of God, to undo the work of the devil.*

And how did Jesus undo Satan's works? By loving us so much that He sacrificed Himself, even to the point of dying for us. Can we love others sufficiently to help them experience Jesus by what we do for them? This is how all of us can be powerful enough to break the traps set by Satan.

---

* Not their real names

---

[1] From Geraldo Rivera's television show *Devil Worship: Exposing Satan's Underground,* aired October 25, 1988.

Chapter 9

Halloween: Why Not Join in the Fun?

For satanists and witches, Halloween is the highest of holy days.

For everyone else, Halloween is a day of lighthearted celebration. By the time October 31 arrives, it's been many months since we've had an excuse to decorate our homes and schools and churches and stores. We delight in the opportunity, so out come the plastic skeletons, cardboard goblins and ceramic Jack-o'-lanterns.

With excitement building, we carve pumpkins, design or choose costumes, create scarecrows, and turn our yards and homes into cemeteries and haunted houses. Winter is approaching, and we want to "Party!" before the dreary, cold days set in. Halloween marks the beginning of festivities that end with New Year's Day.

Everyone knows it's a children's holiday, almost as exciting as Christmas. Then why do so many *adults* participate? Why do stores stock shelves full of witch potholders, jack-o'-lantern cookie jars, black cat candle holders, and goblin door-knob covers?

"It's no longer a children's holiday," commented Jack Sheehan, owner of a costume shop in upstate New York. "The majority of dollars are spent on adults."

Stores that sell seasonal merchandise make twenty-five percent of their annual sales from the celebration of Halloween. According to Hallmark Cards, Inc., in 1988, Americans mailed 28 million Halloween cards. About $300 million was spent on costumes. In 1989, people spent $400 million on costumes. Fifty million adults attended Halloween parties, which is an increase of twenty-five percent since the mid-1980's. The total Halloween business approached $800 million.

By 1996, $800 million was spent on candy alone. Altogether, the purchase of Halloween-related items amounted to about $2.5 billion. More paper and plastic accessories were sold for this day than any other holiday.

"It's the second largest adult party-giving occasion in the United States, bested only by New Year's Eve, "said Hallmark's spokesman, Michael DeMent. And Mark P. Beige, president of the nation's largest costume manufacturer, Rubies Costumes, said, "It has almost taken the status of a U.S. Mardi Gras."

Has interest in Halloween increased because of the growing influence of the occult? The correlation isn't readily visible. On the surface, Halloween seems popular because it provides an opportunity for fantasy.

"The society we live in today," said Philip Morris, head of the costume manufacturing company Morris Costumes, "is a very fast-moving, rapid society. [Halloween] is an opportunity to go back to our childhood . . . to a time when we think that life was a lot easier. It also gives us an opportunity to be anything that we want to be for that one day."

"Everyone wants to fulfill their fantasies," said Eugene DeTone, owner of a costume store in New Jersey. "And what better day than October thirty-one? It's the only day you can get away with it."

Some of us take on the identities of kings and princesses, gorillas and clowns, T.V. characters and legendary heroes. But look at how many choose to be witches and ghosts, devils and vampires! Horror is more popular than heroes. The rule seems to be "the gorier the better." In 1988, Morris Costumes manufactured 60,000 Freddy Krueger masks and could have sold twice as many. This epitome of evil from the *Nightmare on Elm Street* movies was the most popular, most talked-about character of the season. In 1994, the best-selling costume was the Michael Meyers character from the *Halloween* movies. And most of the people pretending to be these psychopathic bad guys are children.

What does this tell us about the meaning of Halloween and why we celebrate it? Why are we so fascinated with death and evil? And why to we encourage it in young, impressionable minds?

In a fourth grade religious education class, one October, a young girl looked up from her drawings of jack-o-lanterns and asked, "What does Halloween have to do with All Saints Day?"

The teacher answered, "The word 'Halloween' comes from 'Hallowed Evening.' Hallowed means holy, so Halloween is a holy evening that prepares us for All Saints Day."

The girl considered the answer. "If Halloween is holy, then God must like devils and spooky games!"

A different but related problem came up in a sixth grade religious education class elsewhere. The class trouble-maker disrupted the lesson by announcing that he performed rituals to Satan. When he described using black candles, a sacrificial cat and a secret place in the woods, the teacher realized that he knew too many details to be making it all up.

That's not what Halloween is supposed to be about. As the eve of All Saints Day — All Hallows' Eve — it should be a time of reverence, a time of learning from those who've gone to Heaven. Perhaps the reason we forget this goes back to its pagan origins and the firm grip the devil has had on this day from the beginning. It was the only pagan holiday that focused on evil. It still is.

Thousands of years ago, while the Celts were still nomads moving westward through Europe, November 1 signalled the need for protection from the harsh forces of winter. As the earth died for the season, people's attention focused on the lord of the dead, *Samhain*.

On the last day of the year, October 31, Samhain

supposedly called together all the souls of wicked people who had died. The barriers between this world and the next supposedly disappeared, allowing for increased psychic phenomena.

To appease the lord of the dead, villagers offered sacrifices by fire. They locked human victims inside wicker cages shaped like animals and monsters, then burned them in bonfires. Human sacrifices on Halloween did not stop until authorities in the Middle Ages discouraged it; they substituted black cats because of their association with witches.

The Druids believed that the dead returned to their former homes while the barriers were down. If the current inhabitants denied them food and shelter, ghosts supposedly would cast evil spells and haunt the people. Here is the beginning of "trick-or-treat." Essentially, it was a bribe to make ghosts leave the people alone.

Even in other parts of the world, these beliefs pervaded. In Mexico, for example, families put food and drink on the table, lit torches and went out to bid the evil spirits enter. Then they worshiped these spirits, praying that they would accept their offerings.

However invited these spirits were, the living did not want them to stay long. To encourage them to leave, the Druid villagers gathered in costumes to escort the spirits out of town. The costumes were supposed to hide their identities so the spirits would not know who wanted them out, lest they should cast a spell.

The Druids also believed that all sorts of supernatural beings — elves, fairies, hobgoblins, witches and warlocks — returned from the nether world. (The term "witches" meant all evil forces that threatened the people. Fairies were originally thought to be superhuman in size and power but supposedly became tiny after Christians came in and sprinkled them with holy water.) In northern England, these entities were blamed for the pranks and practical jokes townspeople played on each other. The evening of October 31 became known as Mischief Night.

Bonfires dotted the hilltops to frighten away the evil spirits. On New Year's Day (November 1), families extinguished their ever-burning household fires to start new ones using embers from the community bonfire. Since fires were vital to life in the home, the period while the hearth was cold was frightening. Hence the fear of evil spirits doing harm was part of this ritual.

Naturally, while all these spirits roamed about, it seemed like the best time for divination. Augury in the form of games was part of the Samhain rituals. People wanted predictions about love, health, prosperity and who was to die in the upcoming year. One of the games that has survived is bobbing for apples. A sixpence was dropped in a tub of water with the apples. Whoever picked up the money with his mouth was supposed to have a financially good year.

Trick-or-treating partly developed in Ireland. On the eve of Samhain, a band of villagers stopped at homes demanding contributions in the name of *Muck Olla*, an ancient Druidic deity. The leader dressed in the costume of a horse, usually a horse's skull and a white robe.

People began to leave goodies on their doorsteps to prevent pranksters from poisoning their wells, stealing their sheep or committing some other wicked deed.

Jack-o'-lanterns were originally hollowed-out turnips or potatoes. Homeowners lit them with candles to ward off evil spirits. Legend says an Irishman named *Jack* tricked the Devil into promising never to come after his soul and so was doomed to wander the earth with his *lantern* forever.

Down through the centuries these rituals continued. Meanwhile, Rome had built its Pantheon in A.D. 100 as a temple to their gods. In A.D. 607 it was given to Pope Boniface IV as a gift. After consecrating it to the Virgin Mary, the Roman Catholics used it to celebrate All Saints

Day on May 13.

Later, Christians evangelized the conquered German Saxons and the Scandinavian Norsemen who still honored Samhain. In A.D. 835, the Church moved All Saints Day to November 1 to depaganize the celebration of the dead and convert it into a holy day. But neither the evil spirits themselves nor the worship of them was easily overcome. The bonfires alone continued until the latter half of the nineteenth century.

It wasn't until the end of the eighteenth century that the morbid focus of the Samhain rituals was transformed into fun celebrations because people began to take spirits and witches less seriously. Halloween had arrived in America with the Scottish settlers, who called it "Snap Apple Night" or "Nutcracker Night." It amounted to little more than parties and occult games of divination. Pumpkins replaced Scottish turnips for Jack-o'-lanterns.

During the potato famine of the 1840s, scores of Irish immigrants came to America and spread throughout the country. They brought with them their superstitions and their belief in hobgoblins, whose mischief was part of the ancient celebrations. The pranks became increasingly destructive. To counter this, school and community groups in the 1920s organized more acceptable forms of fun. Today we follow their guidelines, but the menace has not stopped. Mischief Night is condoned by parents who otherwise would not allow their children to vandalize other people's property. And we fear for our young trick-or-treaters. Parents must accompany the little ones to prevent abductions and then carefully examine the goodies in search of hidden needles and poison.

These modern "pranks" should be enough to make us think twice about this holiday, but shouldn't we also be concerned about Halloween's beginnings? In England, they virtually ignore Halloween because it is a Witches' Sabbat.

Many who don't want to give up Halloween are quick

to point out that we no longer celebrate Halloween for the same reasons as the ancient Celts and Druids. They say there can't be anything wrong with going to parties and wearing costumes. We certainly don't worship the Lord of the Dead!

Or do we? Perhaps we're honoring him without realizing it.

Samhain may have been Satan himself, or at least a powerful demon. The Druids thought of him as a god. In 1 *Corinthians* 10:20 (RSV) we find out what pagan "gods" really are: *What pagans sacrifice they offer to demons and not to God.* Paul went on to warn, in verses 20-22, that God wants us to avoid all involvement with these gods:

> *I do not want you to be partners with demons . .*
> *. You cannot partake of the table of the Lord and*
> *the table of demons. Shall we provoke the Lord*
> *to jealousy? Are we stronger than he?*

Celebrating Halloween is sharing at the table of demons and proof of this is all the focus on fear and horror and evil. The way we glamorize it appears that we're in love with fear or worshipping horror.

Consider the increased interest in the occult around Halloween. This holiday invites us to communicate with spirits through seances, Ouija boards and the like. It makes us more curious about ghosts, witches and Satan. That's exactly what demons want! And because we have so much "fun" with evil, it's no wonder that Satan worship increases this time of year. The Connecticut State Police, for instance, have publicly noted that satanic activity is most common around Halloween.

Do we really want to have a part in this?

Demons have always been involved in Halloween. Fear started the ancient festivities. Rather than trusting in a loving God who could protect them during the long, harsh winter, the people feared the evil forces and invented ways to placate them. Satan's influence was also present in the human sacrifices. And the divination games and the vandalism were certainly not of God.

That eventually only satanists and witches took Halloween seriously says something about its true meaning. As Satan's high holy day, his worshippers believe it's a night when the spirit world has special powers. And for witches, it is still New Year's Eve, a sabbat that marks the beginning of death and destruction. Not much has changed in the way witches and satanists celebrate Halloween.

Of course, most Americans do not think of Halloween the way the ancient pagans did, but the emotions of Samhain worship are still with us. Horror movies are especially popular during October, with more new ones coming out at that time than in any other season. Normally benign television shows dwell on ghosts and witches. People transform attics into haunted houses and yards into cemeteries, complete with peeled grapes for eyeballs and ketchup for blood, all in an attempt to frighten "victims" who pass through.

Why would God approve of anything that promotes fear and horror?

The youth of today are especially vulnerable to Halloween's occultic influences and its focus on death, thanks to the popularity of heavy metal music. Much of it blatantly promotes an obsession with the satanic and an unhealthy preoccupation with death. Children are, by nature, great imitators. Should we wonder, then, why the teen suicide rate is so high?

Since 1960, the teen suicide rate has more than tripled; since 1950, it has increased more than 400%. One out of every 12 high school students tried suicide in 1991, and 27% seriously contemplated it. Both the *National Education Association* and the *American Medical Association* have pointed to popular music as a significant contributing factor in this crisis.

Can there be any good in promoting horror? Psychologically speaking, scaring people and exposing ourselves to make-believe horror gives us a sense — however false — of controlling our anxieties. But there is a better way to control anxiety. We can turn to Christ for help because, as it says in 1 *John* 4:16, 18 (NJB), He drives out all fear:

> *God is love, and whoever remains in love remains in God and God in him. In love there is no room for fear, but perfect love drives out fear, because fear implies punishment and whoever is afraid has not come to perfection in love.*

Hans Holzer, the "Ghost Hunter," has said that Halloween is "a time to rejoice, really, that you are in the physical world and haven't gone to the next one." Obviously, he thinks life in the hereafter is not something to look forward to. However, as Paul said in *Philippians* 1:21, 23 (NJB): *"Death would be a positive gain . . . I want to be gone and to be with Christ, and this is by far the stronger desire."*

Halloween works against the joy-filled, fearless life we can have with Jesus Christ. In 1988, a psychology professor from the State University at Cobleskill, New York, invited his students to a Black Mass for Halloween. "It was for fun," he said afterwards. "It was to get them off campus and to get them away from all of the [Halloween] drinking and partying."

A few students were frightened by the way the professor talked about it, and called the police. When the police arrived at the Black Mass, they witnessed more than fifty students wearing black robes, chanting and carrying torches and candles.

The students were preparing for a human sacrifice. One young man raised a sword into the air, but before he could plunge it into the victim, the police rushed in with their weapons drawn. It turned out the "sword" was a sharpened stick.

"Somebody almost got killed," said the Schoharie

County district attorney. If not by sacrifice, then by police-men ready to shoot to stop what seemed to be a murder.

For the sake of Halloween "fun," the professor had tried to scare his students. He didn't inform them the Black Mass wasn't real until "after everyone was properly frightened," he said.

Why? Why try to scare them with something as im-moral as a satanic ritual? Why expose them to this, the darkest side of the occult, at an age when young people are most likely to be curious about it?

Closer to home, why do we take our own children to contrived haunted houses? When a toddler goes in smil-ing and comes out crying, what does that tell us? There is already too much in life that frightens youngsters and leaves lasting scars. Why deliberately give them more?

And why intentionally expose them to evil? Why encourage our children to develop an interest in ghosts, witches, vampires and Freddy Kruegers? That's what we do when we allow them to wear these costumes. When a child says, "I want to be a devil for Halloween," we should ask, "Is this their role model?" Why don't they prefer being a president or astronaut or legendary hero? And since this is the eve of All Saints Day, why don't they want to be St. Francis of Assisi or the saint after whom they were named?

Much of this is our own fault. We set the example. We can either show our children it's okay to pretend to be evil, or we can show them it's more fun to pretend to be a famous hero who does the work of God.

Every time Halloween is celebrated, Satan wins a victory and the world grows darker because it over-shadows All Saints Day, which was supposed to replace it. Why do we want to help him continue this victory? Why aren't we more willing to turn the light of Christ onto this holiday and reveal it for what it really is?

Our participation tells our children, our neighbors, our relatives and our co-workers that we accept and approve of the dark world of the occult. Then, if they become interested in or continue to practice the occult, we're partly to blame. And since the practices of Satanism increase this time of year, we're also encouraging teenagers to explore devil worship. Do we really want to be part of this?

Yes, it's difficult swimming against the tide of Halloween's popularity. Most of us who feel uncomfortable about Halloween nevertheless continue to join in because we're concerned about what others might think of us. It's peer pressure. But this means we're in bondage to fear. We're afraid to take a stand, we're afraid of being rejected. We need to ask God for the boldness—I call it "holy boldness"—to be a true follower of Him and His ways.

Imagine yourself carrying a heavy load of garbage on your back down a long road. You move slowly and your stooped shoulders ache. Jesus meets you and takes that load. You stand up straight. You have new energy. You can dance and skip and travel easily. But then someone else comes along and gives you another sack of garbage. Would you take it?

If you turn away from the occult to get closer to God, why go back to the things of the devil on Halloween? Paul spoke of this in *Romans* 12:2 (NJB):

> *Do not model your behaviour on the contemporary world, but let the renewing of your minds transform you, so that you may discern for yourselves what is the will of God — what is good and acceptable and mature.*

In *Ephesians* 5:8-11 (NAB), Paul reiterated this by telling us to reject the darkness of the world's ways so that we won't extinguish the light of Christ:

> *There was a time when you were darkness, but now you are light in the Lord . . . live as children of light. Light produces every kind of goodness and justice and truth. Be correct in*

*your judgment of what pleases the Lord. Take
no part in vain deeds done in darkness but;
rather, condemn them.*

Once we stop celebrating Halloween, people do ask
why. That's our opportunity to share what we've learned
about the occult and about God's superior gifts. They may
huff in disbelief, but at least we've planted a seed. Then if
we put it in God's hands, and we find opportunities to
deliver His love to them, we can expect Him to till the soil
and water the so the idea can begin to grow.

In our boycott of Halloween, we needn't stop celebrating altogether. We can create a new holiday. In San
Jose, California, for example, the townspeople make
October 31 a Fall Festival. Satanic costumes are discouraged, and trick-or-treating is replaced by parties at schools
and churches. Likewise, the schools in Tallahassee,
Florida, and a growing number of other places have replaced Halloween with Harvest Festivals.

Some communities are keeping Halloween but doing
away with the focus on horror. In Harlingen, Texas, the
school superintendent responded to parents' anxieties by
telling principals to "review their practices and if they had
anything that depicted blood and gore, to try to eliminate
that." In Waukesha, Wisconsin, students have been
forbidden to dress in costumes that depict characters from
violent movies. Although this isn't enough to overcome
everything that's wrong with Halloween, it helps.

An elementary school in Amarillo, Texas, created
Pumpkin Fun Day because other schools in the area had
dropped Halloween carnivals. In Levy County, Florida,
the superintendent of schools took it a step further because parents expressed concern that Halloween encourages occult activities. He ruled out all Halloween decora-
tions or parties in the schools.

We can all go to our school superintendents and community leaders to express our objections to Halloween.

We can create our own alternative, one that focuses on harvest. We can decorate our homes and schools and workplaces with *uncarved* pumpkins, Indian corn, gourds, and other harvest symbols. We can wear costumes that represent good instead of evil.

In churches, the emphasis can be on the harvest of souls, using Jesus' parable of the sowing of seeds among weeds (*Matthew* 13:24-30, 37-43), in which the harvest represents the end of the world when God will separate the good crop from the bad and destroy the weeds of the enemy.

One church in Moline, Illinois, has converted the "haunted house" idea into a "heavenly house." The different rooms depict Bible stories from *Genesis to Revelation*. They open it to the community and they replace fear and horror with the love and promises of Jesus Christ.

Most people don't stop to think about the true meaning of Halloween. Perhaps we don't know God very well, or we don't believe Satan exists, or we don't realize we're helping Satan celebrate his sacred day. But our ignorance does not cancel out the homage we give the devil.

It doesn't matter what we as individuals think of this holiday. What's important is the message we give about fear and horror and evil. What's important is how our participation—or refusal to participate—affects others. What's important is what God thinks of Halloween. It's Satan's favorite day of the year because so many of us help him use it to attract people away from Jesus.

Halloween is an example of how Christians have been too silent and accepting of the occult. We must wake up to the fact that we are fighting a spiritual battle.

Chapter 10

Protection From Demons

Satan thought he had won a victory when I lost my relationship with God. He saw me stop praying. He saw my Bible collect dust. He saw me stop going to church. He inspired the thought: "If I go to church just on Easter and Christmas, I'll be one of those hypocrites!" He heard me decide, "I'll stay home and honor those holidays my own way."

But Jesus didn't give up on me. He never stops trying to win us back. Pope John Paul II assures us of this in *Towards the Third Millennium*:

> Going in search of man through his Son, God wishes to persuade man to abandon the paths of evil which lead him farther and farther afield. "Making him abandon" those paths means making man understand that he is taking the wrong path; it means overcoming the evil which is everywhere found. . . . Overcoming evil: this is the meaning of Redemption. This is brought about in the sacrifice of Christ, by which man redeems the debt of sin and is reconciled to God.

God knew just how to encourage me to abandon the path I was on. I suspect He sent a divine messenger (an angel) to inspire an old friend to call me. When my telephone rang, the voice that greeted me belonged to someone I hadn't heard from in a long time—Father Ed Nichols. As we renewed our acquaintance, God inspired Father Ed to invite himself over for a week of his vacation time, just a few weeks hence. Yes, it was short notice. And yes, he was being rather bold. But when God implements a strategy, everything falls into place. God probably even surrounded him with protective angels to prevent Satan from blocking whatever God was doing.

During the week of Father Ed's visit, he never mentioned the occult. He knew of my involvement in it and he knew it was dangerous. He also knew I wasn't going to church. But instead of condemning me, he uplifted me. He revealed Jesus to me by caring about me and my husband. As a result, our discussions resurrected my long-buried desire for God's love.

Then Father Ed left for a Christian conference halfway across the country. I knew I had to go, too.

"If I don't go," I told Ralph, "I may lose whatever new start I've had this week."

Although this trip would mean being apart for the first time since our wedding day, Ralph agreed I should go. But Satan doesn't like to lose his prisoners of war. The demons who'd been influencing my life wanted to stop me from going to the conference. They knew it would undo everything they had accomplished through the occult. So they battled to keep me home.

First they manipulated my insecurities. I didn't think our little bank account could afford the cost of the plane fare. But Ralph told me that since this trip was for the sake of my relationship with the Lord, God would make sure our finances would survive the dip. I was also very doubtful that I could get the five days off from my job. Ralph suggested I ask for the Lord's help and try.

To my surprise, my boss agreed to the time off. I bought the plane tickets and packed. Then the demons tried to manipulate Ralph's insecurities. When it was time for me to leave for the airport, Ralph said: "Don't go."

"Huh?"

Fear and uncertainty had overcome him. We argued about it as I watched the clock. Soon the plane would depart, but I couldn't change Ralph's mind. It took off without me.

With their victory won, the demons relaxed. Ralph began to think more clearly.

"Perhaps you should have gone," he said.

"It's too late now," I groaned. "The next plane doesn't leave till tomorrow." I couldn't see the point in spending so much money for only part of a conference.

Then it seemed like an angel whispered an idea into Ralph's ear. Ralph said: "Missing one day is better than missing the whole thing."

He convinced me. I went to what was left of the conference and recommited my life to Christ. By the time I returned home, God had filled me with His Holy Spirit. I had a new future. Satan and his cohorts had lost.

Ralph and I were not aware of angels helping us. We didn't even realize that Satan had been involved until later. The fact is, the spiritual world — although invisible — is real. Much happens that we can't see; much goes on to help or hinder us that we know nothing about. But every day, a battle between demons and angels, Satan and Christ is being waged. And we are the booty they're fighting for.

This is a hard truth to accept. We don't want to believe that demons fight against us or use us in their battles. The idea scares us. It means life isn't as simple as we thought. It means we're vulnerable; there's much we don't know because we can't see it. It means we'll have to put on spiritual armor and pick up God's weapons and use them.

We can no longer sit back and say, "Anything that happens is God's will," or "That's just the way the world is, so I can't do anything about it," or "This problem is too big for me, and it won't go away, so I'll just run away from it." It is not God's will for bad things to happen. We can do something about evil. We need to turn the bad things over to God to make good come out of them, and we must learn how to overcome evil, but that takes commitment! Fear and apathy are tools of the devil. If we fear demons, their powers seem stronger than ours. If we choose to believe there is no war, we stand on the battlefield unarmed. Either way, we easily become Satan's victims.

It doesn't have to be this way. We can win every battle if we first prepare ourselves. We can use divine power, knowledge of Satan's methods, knowledge of his weaknesses, the spiritual armor God has provided for us, the Blood of the Lamb, and our spiritual gifts.

Divine Power

By our action or inaction, we decide the outcome of the spiritual battles that are waged around us. Angels are fighting the enemy on our behalf, but there is only so much they can do without our involvement. God gave us a free will. We can either ask for God's power or remain vulnerable. We can let the enemy wound us or we can send him fleeing. The Bible tells us how to chase him off in *James* 4:8 (RSV):

> *Submit yourselves therefore to God. Resist the*
> *devil and he will flee from you.*

There is no need to fear demons, no matter how they might attack us. When we put ourselves in Jesus' hands, conquering the enemy becomes easy. That's because Jesus already conquered Satan. He won our victories for us by taking our sins to that painful cross and overcoming death on Easter morning. Resisting the devil by ourselves is difficult. Unless our lives are filled with God, Satan only laughs at our attempts and then attacks again.

Jon K. experienced this first hand. He told me, "Anyone who is not reading the Word of God and is not praying without ceasing is very open to the subtle arrows of Satan and his demons."

Jon had become a Christian at age sixteen and wanted to devote his life to God, but during college he stopped praying and reading the Bible. To feed his spiritual hunger, he began to read books on the occult. He said, "I found that the philosophy they taught allowed me to seek after money and pleasure without a serious thought of the Lord of Lords." The path led quickly downhill into fornication, alcohol abuse and other problems.

In his search for God, he grabbed onto the New Age "salvation" of a universal religion. In the process, he discovered that Christianity was the only religion that didn't fit neatly together with the rest, and he wanted to make it fit. He said, "I knew I needed to know more if I were to make Christianity compatible."

While reading a Christian book, everything he used to believe came back to him. He asked Jesus to become the most important part of his life again. Reflecting on why he had been drawn into the occult and other sins despite his strong love for God, he said, "Because I had not been studying God's Word and praying, when I was tempted, I was enticed away."

We are all tempted by demons. We have to cling to Jesus and follow His example of how to live in order for Him to lift us out of the Enemy's reach. *James* 4:8-10 (NJB) tells us:

> *The nearer you go to God, the nearer God will come to you. . . . Humble yourselves before the Lord and he will lift you up.*

This is what Satan wants to prevent. The closer we get to God, the farther we get from Satan's influence. Satan's power is puny compared to God's. Demonic power is no threat to those who rely on the Holy Spirit. What makes Satan seem strong is first of all his lie that he is greater than God, and secondly, our weak, half-hearted attempt to push Satan away and grip onto God's mighty hand. Let's face it, God is not as much a part of our lives as we need Him to be.

We were all born on a battlefield. The earth is where a multi-millennia fight between God and Satan is being played out. The war started when Satan rebelled, requiring God to cast him out of Heaven. Eventually, when God is finished working His plans on earth, Christ will return in glory with an army of angels to end the war. This is foretold in 2 *Thessalonians* 2:8 (TLB):

> *This wicked one will appear, whom the Lord Jesus will . . . destroy by his presence when he returns.*

Rev. Billy Graham has pointed out:

> In his warfare against God, Satan uses the human race, which God created and loved. So God's forces of good and Satan's forces of evil have been engaged in a deadly conflict from the dawn of our history. . . . We will find no final solution to the world's great problems until this spiritual warfare has been settled. And it will be settled in the last war of history — Armageddon. Then Christ and His angelic armies will be the victor![1]

Until then, we can either ignore the battle and be its victims, join the enemy's troops and lose Christ, or fight on God's side with the power of Christ and become victors.

We can't avoid the battle. Even if we try to ignore it, the enemy will still come at us. If we try to walk away from it, pretending it doesn't exist, we get stabbed in the back. Evil triumphs when the good do nothing.

Know the Enemy's Methods

To protect ourselves in battle, it helps to know how the enemy attacks. Here are some of his favorite strategies:

1. He gets people to attribute all spiritual experiences to God.

2. He twists and perverts Scripture.

3. He makes life so comfortable, we see no need for Jesus.

4. He gives us reasons to doubt God's promises, so he can separate us from God's love and power.

5. He bombards our minds with thoughts, desires, and motives that lead us away from God.

6. He feeds us fear and other negative emotions that keep us from knowing the joy of Christ.

7. He gives us illnesses and diseases, to discourage us and blind us or deafen us to God's Word.

8. He desensitizes us to immorality through such repeated exposure to violent or morally-lacking television shows.

9. He tempts us to sin. (However, God does not permit him to test us beyond our powers to resist.)

10. He accuses us, making us feel guilty or unforgivable or unworthy of God's love.

11. He puts us in bondage, i.e., he enslaves us to prevent us from receiving the abundance Christ came to give us.

12. He possesses us, if possible, occupying our whole lives to keep Christ out.

Once we become aware of the enemy's methods, we can recognize his attacks and fight back. There is power in such knowledge.

Know the Enemy's Weaknesses

In any battle between nations, "intelligence" plays a key role. We gain a strategic advantage if we discover the enemy's weaknesses.

Satan knows this. He sends out secret agents to observe us and learn where we're most vulnerable. They study our habits, our concerns and our interests to see what they can use to try to corrupt us. Armed with this information, they tempt us in ways they think might defeat us. If, for example, they find out we like to help friends solve their problems, they might give us the gift of fortune telling, to prevent us from leading our friends to God's help.

Where we are weak, we are vulnerable. Any part of our lives that is not under God's protection is open for attack. But the same holds true for demons. Since Satan is completely outside God's protection, he is extremely vulnerable. We can easily overcome him.

What other "intelligence" can we gather?

Most of what we hear about the enemy (except by means of God's Word) is propaganda and deception. Demons hide their true characters. They don't want us to know their weaknesses, so they disguise themselves as whatever will give them respect or fear. For example, have you ever heard someone speak very authoritatively, with such confidence that you start believing that what they said must be true? They could be totally wrong, but they speak with so much assurance, they even convince themselves. That's the way demons sometimes work. They mess with our minds using techniques that make the lies sound true, and thus fool us into believing what we would not otherwise believe.

But, the good news is: We can unmask the enemy by studying the Word of God. The Bible tells us everything we need to know about the enemy. It tells us how to spot his battle tactics. It also tells us what the truth is so we can recognize the lies.

Here is the enemy exposed: Despite what Satan would have us believe, he is not God. He is just a fallen angel. Therefore, he does not have God's three main attributes: omniscience, omnipotence, and omnipresence.

1. Satan, like every demon, is not **omniscient** or all-knowing. He cannot read our minds; he learns our intentions, our feelings, and our weak points by what we express visibly and verbally. His perceptions are limited; for example, he wanted people to kill Jesus because he failed to realize that Christ's death would mean his own defeat. He cannot see the future, although he can make some good guesses because of his high intelligence (here I use "intelligence" to mean both smartness and spywork).

2. Satan is not **omnipotent**, all-powerful. The supernatural powers he uses against us, as well as the supernatural gifts he offers through the occult, are limited. He cannot work miracles that out-do God's, as proven time and again in both the Old and New Testaments. He cannot overpower us unless we let him. When we command him and the other demons — in Jesus' name — to leave us, it's impossible for them to stay.

3. Satan cannot be everywhere at once, or **omnipresent**. He is a finite being. He sends out his demons to spread his influence around, and they, too, are limited. There are more angels than demons, so even with his entire army at work, he cannot be fighting all the time, everywhere. He may be more active in our lives than we care to realize, but once we start thinking he's involved in everything, we're giving him more credit than he's due.

St. Paul said in *Ephesians* 6:12 (TLB):

> *We are not fighting against people made of flesh and blood, but against persons without bodies — the evil rulers of the unseen world, those mighty satanic beings and great evil princes of darkness . . . and against huge numbers of wicked spirits.*

We live in a world of death, germs, tornadoes, poisonous snakes and all forms of destruction. Because humankind, like Satan, has disobeyed the Creator from the beginning, we cannot live in a trouble-free Garden of Eden. We live in Satan's domain and need Jesus to help us rise above it (*Gal.* 1:4).

Therefore, while some of our troubles are direct attacks by demons, others happen simply because we live in the midst of demons. For example, an evil spirit could directly cause our death by making a snake bite us while we hike through the woods, or we may cause it ourselves by choosing to walk where snakes nest.

Since Jesus conquered Satan when He died on the cross and then rose from the dead, we can ask Him to help us with the troubles that come from living in Satan's world. Remember that St. Paul was bitten by a poisonous snake once (*Acts* 28:3-5), but because of his faith in Jesus, he came to no harm (see *Mark* 16-18). This doesn't mean that we can carelessly fool with snakes, thinking that Jesus will keep their poison from killing us. We need to combine Christ's help with a healthy dose of the common sense given to us by our Father.

Neither should the enemy's interference in our lives make us worried and fearful. We can use knowledge of his tactics and weaknesses to figure out how to fight back and win, but we should not dwell on the evil he might do. Whenever we face troubles, our focus should be on the God who saves us, not on whether Satan is making things go wrong.

There are spiritual battles to fight every day. It's important to know this so we can rely on our armor, pick up our weapons, and live victoriously. We don't want to glorify Satan by giving him all our attention. We can take as our example the Bible. While it does teach about demons, its main concern is the Gospel of the love of God. It shows us that our eyes should always be on Jesus.

The Armor of God

We're told in *Ephesians* 6:10, 11 (NAB) that God has provided a very special armor for us to wear as we fight the enemy:

> *Finally, draw your strength from the Lord and his mighty power. Put on the armor of God so that you may be able to stand firm against the tactics of the devil.*

So essential is this, Pope Paul VI quoted it in an important document of Vatican Council II in 1964, the *Dogmatic Constitution on the Church*: "We strive therefore to please God in all things (see 2 *Cor.* 5:9) and we put on the armor of God, that we may be able to stand against the wiles of the devil."

If we're trying to get rid of occult influences, if we're trying to mend a failing marriage, if we're trying to find a better job, or if we're facing disease, financial problems, bad habits, runaway children—if we're facing any kind of struggle, Satan wants us to lose. He hates us. He's extremely jealous because he knows how much God loves us. He'll do anything to separate us from that love.

However, if we have Jesus, he can't succeed. See what the Bible says about this in *Romans* 8:37-39 (NJB):

> *We come through all these things triumphantly victorious, by the power of him who loved us. For I am certain of this: neither death nor life, nor angels, nor principalities, nothing already in existence and nothing still to come, nor any power, nor the heights nor the depths, nor any created thing whatever, will be able to come between us and the love of God, known to us in Christ Jesus our Lord.*

To defeat the enemy, we need "the power of him who loved us." Our own power is not enough. We must use God's protection, the armor that comes from God's Kingdom. St. Paul told us how in *Ephesians* 6:14-17 (NJB):

> *So stand your ground, with truth a belt round your waist, and uprightness a breastplate, wearing for shoes on your feet the eagerness to*

> *spread the gospel of peace and always carrying the shield of faith so that you can use it to quench the burning arrows of the Evil One. And then you must take salvation as your helmet and the sword of the Spirit, that is, the word of God.*

We receive all these pieces of armor when we commit our lives to Christ. By clothing ourselves with Christ's truth, uprightness, eagerness to spread the gospel, faith, salvation and Word, we protect ourselves from the enemy.

1. *The belt of truth* helps us identify Satan's lies and deceptions. We learn the truth by studying the Bible. We discover: I shouldn't listen to my doubts about God; God is who He says He is, I am what God says I am, God does what he says He'll do, and I can do whatever God says I can do.

2. *The breastplate of uprightness* is God's righteousness. When the Holy Spirit lives within us, He helps us recognize sinful desires, wrong thoughts and bad motives. Uprightness overcomes Satan's temptations.

3. *The shoes of evangelization* are offensive weapons. We win battles and break Satan's power every time we help someone grow closer to God. Christ's shoes give us the same boldness He used to spread God's truth.

4. *The shield of faith* is our most important protection. It protects us from the burning arrows of doubt. Jesus told us that if our faith is the size of a mustard seed — one of the tiniest of seeds — we can move mountains (*Matt.* 17:20). Since faith is a gift from the Holy Spirit (1 *Cor.* 12:9), we have all *His* faith available to us. That's a lot of faith!

5. *The helmet of salvation* covers our heads. This is a very important piece of armor, because the most common area where the enemy attacks is our minds. Christ's act of salvation — sacrificing His life for each of us — rescued us from sin and death. Knowing this protects our minds from doubts and despair. Trusting in it helps us win both

physical and spiritual victories.

6. *The Word of God* is our strongest weapon. It cuts through the deceptions of the enemy and slashes his power. We wield it by knowing what the Word of God (the Bible) says, understanding Who the Word of God (Jesus) is, and by speaking the Word to God as prayer, to ourselves as an aid in applying it, and to demons as a sword to make them flee.

The Blood of the Lamb

When Jesus suffered for our sins, He shed a lot of blood. The Roman soldiers whipped Him until His skin was raw. The crown of thorns pierced His head in many places. Did you ever cut your forehead? The tiniest wound bleeds profusely. And the spikes nailed into His hands and feet rubbed the flesh as He hung; the blood had no time to coagulate.

He did that for you. And me. "He merited for us life by the free shedding of His own blood. In Him God reconciled us to Himself and among ourselves; from bondage to the devil and sin He delivered us," it says in the Vatican Council II document *Pastoral Constitution on the Church in the Modern World*. In other words, Jesus willingly shed His blood for you and me by sacrificing His life as a retribution for our sins. Since our sins keep us from being closer to our Divine Father, Jesus' blood heals our relationship with God.

Christ's blood purifies us when we ask for the Father's forgiveness. It protects us from guilt. Pope John Paul II explains this in his encyclical letter *The Holy Spirit in the Life of the Church and the World: Hebrews* 9:14 "says that this 'blood purifies the conscience.' It therefore, so to speak, opens to the Holy Spirit the door into man's inmost being, namely into the sanctuary of human consciences."

When this happens, demons cannot bear to be near us. What a powerful protection! *Revelation* 12:11 (NJB) describes the defeat of Satan during the final battle:

> *They have triumphed over him by the blood of*
> *the Lamb and by the word to which they bore*
> *witness.*

The Lamb is a beautiful image of Christ because it symbolizes His sacrificial offering for our sins. "The Word" also refers to Christ, God's message of salvation. Both we and the angels triumph because Christ shed His blood for humankind. To use this protection, we can ask Jesus to cover us with His blood. This is a symbolic—but very real—way of asking for Christ's victory over Satan.

I rely on the protection of His blood often. A good example of how well this works is the story I call "The Neighborhood Feud." For several months, two families had been fighting to keep a third family from moving in. Hostility had escalated beyond hope of forgiveness.

When Ralph and I moved into this neighborhood and learned of the feud, we began to pray for a miracle of peace. First, we told the demons involved to get out. Then we asked Jesus to cover the three houses and their families with His precious blood, and we prayed for this as often as we felt it was necessary. Gradually, the arguments diminished. The neighbors began to treat each other like neighbors instead of enemies. The true enemy had fled.

Spiritual Gifts

God not only gives us armor for winning spiritual battles, He also gives us spiritual abilities, as explained in Vatican Council II's *Decree on the Apostolate of the Laity*:

> The Holy Spirit Who sanctifies the people
> of God. . . gives the faithful special gifts
> also (see 1 *Cor.* 12:7), "allotting them to
> everyone according as He wills" (1 *Cor.*
> 12:11) in order that individuals. . . may also

be "good stewards of the manifold grace of God" (1 *Peter* 4:10), to build up the whole body in charity (see *Eph.* 4:16). From the acceptance of these charisms, including those which are more elementary, there arise for each believer the right and duty to use them. . . for the good of men and the building up of the Church, in the freedom of the Holy Spirit. . . .

St. Paul listed the most important gifts in 1 *Corinthians* 12:8-10 (NJB):

1. *The gift of utterance expressing wisdom:* When Satan attacks, the Holy Spirit can give you a word of wisdom on how to respond. It was this gift that helped Ralph and me know how to chase the spirits of the feud out of the neighborhood.

2. *The gift of utterance expressing knowledge:* The Holy Spirit can provide helpful bits of information. For example, a woman being prayed over for crippling arthritis received only slight improvement. One of those praying had an inner sense that the woman needed to forgive her sister. Prior to this, they didn't even know she had a sister. When this word of knowledge was shared, the woman admitted having a sister to whom she had refused to speak for thirty years. When she forgave her for whatever had caused the separation, the arthritis disappeared.

3. *The gift of faith:* Faith is part of the armor of Christ mentioned in Ephesians. As a gift from God, it empowers us. When we have doubts, it does not mean we don't have faith; it means we're not choosing to give God our trust. At these times we can pray, "Jesus, you be my trust." Trust releases the power of faith.

4. *The gift of healing:* Illness weakens God's human army. Since our hands serve as Christ's hands, He can use us to provide healing. Soon after I started writing this

book, for instance, I felt the early symptoms of a cold. I stopped typing, put my hands over my sinuses, and bound Satan from interfering. I also cast out the spirit of infirmity, asked Jesus to fill me with His health, and thanked Him. The symptoms disappeared immediately.

5. *The working of miracles:* If we need to, we can call upon God's power to frustrate Satan's plans. God has started our car when it died from wet wires on the way to an important ministry meeting. He found us a baby-sitter when no one was available so we could attend a Christian conference. I could write a whole book on what He has done!

6. *The gift of prophecy:* We can learn God's battle plans or hear His pep talks through this gift. Prophecy, in the Biblical sense, is any Word from the Holy Spirit. Sometimes it foretells the future, but more often it teaches us things the Lord wants us to know.

7. *The power of distinguishing spirits:* Satan's deceptions need not fool us. We can know what comes from the Spirit of God, what comes from our own human spirits, and what comes from the evil spirits of the enemy. Then, we can respond accordingly.

8. *The gift of different tongues:* As with all spiritual gifts, Satan sometimes counterfeits the ability to speak a foreign language not known by the speaker. But the gift of tongues that comes from God, as mentioned in the Bible (1 *Cor.* 12:10), is a manifestation of the Holy Spirit indicating that He is present and that we have submitted our will to His. When God inspires one person to use this gift in a group setting, it means He wants to say something to which we'd better listen. It must then be followed by the next gift.

9. *The interpretation of tongues:* This is a translation of the unknown language spoken to a group of worshipers. It works like the gift of prophecy.

These gifts are meted out according to God's wisdom,

our needs and our willingness to use them. The more we are filled with God's Spirit and use the gifts to help others grow closer to Him, the stronger these gifts become. And, like the gifts of music or mathematical prowess, we improve them with practice.

It's important to remember that these gifts work best in or with community. We find a lot of protection in Christian communities, which is why St. Paul wrote in 1 *Corinthians* 12:7 (TLB):

> *The Holy Spirit displays God's power through each of us as a means of helping the entire church.*

When stronger trust is needed to believe that God is truly helping us during bad times, we can ask our friends to pray for us. When we have trouble figuring out what demonic influences are keeping us from experiencing the full power of God, we can go to someone whose gift of knowledge is well developed. Or if we're not sure whether something we want to get involved in is of God, we can talk to someone who has the gift of discernment.

Our success in fighting Satan depends on our ability to recognize his works, our knowledge of how to defeat him, and our willingness to expel him from troubling situations.

---

[1] Billy Graham, *Angels: God's Secret Agents*, Carmel, NY: Guideposts Associates, Inc., 1975, pp.64-65.

Chapter 11

Supernatural Warriors

It takes supernatural power to defeat demons. The battlefield is no place for civilians. We must put on the armor of Christ, pick up our weapons, and become warriors. We win victories by asking Jesus Christ to be our Commander-in-Chief, by renouncing Satan, and by using the weapons God gives us. The more we allow Jesus to transform our lives — our habits, feelings, desires, talents, etc. — the more victorious each day becomes. But whenever we compromise God's ways with the world's ways, we weaken our defense.

After I rediscovered my desire for God, recommiting my life to Him was not enough. I still had to get rid of the demons to which I'd exposed myself. Any hold they had on me would block the fullness of God's power.

I had come back from the Christian conference a changed person, but I still carried much of the old baggage. I started going to church every Sunday and joined a prayer group to help my growth. By exposing myself to the Word of God and the witness of other Christians, I learned a few surprises about my occult beliefs.

One by one, the Holy Spirit showed me scriptures that refuted each occult practice. So one by one, I renounced my occult involvements. I asked Jesus to replace them with His presence. Gradually, the baggage shrank.

I gave up the load of occult sins that had been weighing down my spiritual life, but I was not yet in the clear. The demons I'd exposed myself to were still around, waiting for the opportunity to snatch me back to the enemy's camp. I needed Jesus to free me from them. I didn't get rid of them alone — one person does not an army make. I turned to a priest for counseling. Through his prayers and the **Sacrament of Reconciliation**, Christ delivered me of all occult bondage.

Deliverance means gaining freedom from demonic influence. It is another word for "healing". It is not exorcism. It is rare for people in our society to need exorcism, because demons have fewer opportunities to possess people when God is a dominant part of the culture. Often, when a preacher or prayer group performs multiple exorcisms in this country, it's probably not real. It is possible that demons are staging (or encouraging the people to stage) the exorcisms in order to increase fear. Few—if any—of the exorcised people may be actually getting a healing from Christ.

Exorcism

Exorcisms are not exclusive to Christianity. They're done by voodoo witch doctors, psychic healers, cult leaders and other practitioners of the occult. They're also done by "Christians" who center entire "ministries" on demon possession.

Satan can even approve of this kind of exorcism because it creates fear. And he knows that as long as the exorcisms aren't centered on Christ, they can't defeat him. As evidenced in the example from *Acts* 19:13-16 (NJB), it is only by Christ's authority that we can be effective:

> *But some itinerant Jewish exorcists too tried pronouncing the name of the Lord Jesus over people who were possessed by evil spirits; they used to say, "I adjure you by the Jesus whose spokesman is Paul." Among those who did this were seven sons of Sceva, a Jewish chief priest. The evil spirit replied, "Jesus I recognize, and Paul I know, but who are you?" And the man with the evil spirit hurled himself at them and overpowered first one and then another, and handled them so violently that they fled from*

that house stripped of clothing and badly mauled.

Exorcism can be dangerous. It is not something to be played with. If you think someone you know is possessed, get help. There are priests in the Roman Catholic Church, for example, who are empowered to do this work, but they only proceed with the guidance and permission of their bishop.

"When a possible demonic intervention is suggested," state the writers of *Christian Faith and Demonology*, "the Church always imposes a critical assessment of the facts." The person who's allegedly possessed is given a battery of psychological tests to determine the true cause of his problems. "It is easy to fall victim to imagination and to allow oneself to be led astray by inaccurate accounts distorted in their transmission and incorrectly interpreted. . . . One must exercise discernment."

The candidate for exorcism is observed for signs of possession. According to the *Rituale Romanum*, these include the ability to a) speak or understand a foreign language never studied; b) foretell future events or show extrasensory awareness of the thoughts and/or actions of those about him, or of distant situations; c) display superhuman strength or manifestations of power beyond the subject's natural age; d) exhibit other phenomena of a particularly vicious nature (such as violent and obscene behavior) which, while in variance with the subject's own personality, suggest demonic intervention.

Other indications could be altered personality, independent voices, abhorrence for religious artifacts, loathing of anything having to do with Christian faith, compulsions to disturb Christian meetings, and impossible physical manifestations including levitation, bloating, and vomiting enormous amounts of foreign matter.

If after much discernment and prayer the attending priests believe it's true possession, and the bishop agrees, the priests must prepare by going on a retreat that includes prayer and fasting. Two priests often share the responsibility for the exorcism. It is difficult to perform it alone.

Deliverance

If a person belongs to Jesus Christ, possession is not possible, but **harassment** is. Demons can attack the parts of our lives that do not belong to God. For example, if we study reincarnation because we enjoy believing it's possible, that interest is outside of God's loving will for us. Therefore, it's outside of God's protection. Demons will jump at that opportunity and attack us with half-truths about Christ's salvation, leading us to eventually believe that people don't need Jesus' sacrifice on the cross.

When they get a grip on our thinking or enslave us by keeping some area of our lives away from God's will (called **bondage**), they gain some control. Resisting is no longer enough to make them flee.

Bondage often reveals itself through irrational fear or anger or guilt, an inability to pray, rejection of God, incurable disease or chronic illness, the tendency to be accident-prone, addictions, mental illness, consistent irrational behavior, etc. Some bondages are very disruptive, as in the case of people who fear leaving home. Some are less obvious, such as feeling unworthy of love.

Discernment is necessary to determine if a problem is due to bondage or something else, such as a chemical imbalance or an overactive imagination. Binding and casting out demons in the name of Jesus Christ should be done only after careful analysis and prayer. If a change then results in the person, you can be sure demons had indeed been at work.

Steps should then be taken to assure that any remaining psychological and spiritual needs are taken care of through normal methods — this is an important and essential follow-up!.

However, if there is no change after the deliverance

expose him to demons, then you know the problem is either psychological or physical. The person should be referred to a competent doctor.

The importance of deliverance should not be taken lightly. Bondage keeps us from living the abundant life Christ came to give us, as indicated by Jesus' words in *John* 10:10 (NJB):

> *The thief* [Satan] *comes only to steal and kill and destroy. I have come so that you may have life and have it to the full.*

Deliverance — breaking free — is expelling demons and persistently transforming our lives until their influence is gone for good.It is a form of healing. It has eight steps:

1. Repent of all occult involvement (or whatever the sin is). If you have the Sacrament of Reconciliation *(Confession)* available, as Roman Catholics do, take advantage of this opportunity to cleanse yourself. Renounce Satan and each area of occult interest. Open yourself to receive the joy of God's forgiveness. For it is written in 1 *John* 1:9 (NJB):

> *If we acknowledge our sins, he is trustworthy and upright, so that he will forgive our sins and will cleanse us from all evil.*

2. Ask Jesus to be the Lord of your life. He assures us in *Luke* 4:18 that He came to set captives free, including the oppressed. But He warned in *Luke* 11:24-26 (NJB) that expelling demons can lead to worse possession:

> *When an unclean spirit goes out of someone it wanders through waterless country looking for a place to rest, and not finding one it says, "I will go back to the home I came from." But on arrival, finding it swept and tidied, it then goes off and brings seven other spirits more wicked than itself, and they go in and set up house*

> *there, and so that person ends up worse off than before.*

It is vital that whenever we get rid of demons, we ask Jesus to fill the now empty "house." Demons cannot return if Christ dwells there. Likewise, if Jesus lives in us, demons must obey our commands. Jesus must always be our partner in expelling evil.

3. Bind Satan in the name of Jesus and command him to go. You can't conquer the enemy's plans unless you first get rid of the commander. Jesus pointed out in *Matthew* 12:29 that no one can "make his way into a strong man's house and plunder his property unless he has first tied up the strong man".

4. Since demons are behind the occult, bind and cast out, also in Jesus' name, the spirits of fortune telling, astrology, or whatever you've been involved with. Tell them to go to the foot of Jesus' cross. Command them not to return to you.

5. Ask God to fill you with His Holy Spirit and to provide His healing. Ask to receive the opposites of everything that was cast out. Until you do this, you're vulnerable. Jesus promised in *John* 16:13, that "When the Spirit of truth comes he will lead you to the complete truth". Roman Catholics have a special Sacrament for this, called the Anointing of the Sick. The priest prays for you to "be delivered from sin and from all temptation." He anoints you with blessed oil (chrism), which is regarded as a protection for your body, soul and spirit.

6. Seek Christian fellowship for prayers and encouragement. At first you may feel as if the bondage still exists. That's because you're used to living with it. You've built ruts in the road through which you journeyed, and travelling in them has become automatic. It takes time to make new ruts. Other Christians can help you get through this and help your faith grow. That's why Paul wrote in 1 *Corinthians* 12:27 (NJB):

> *Now Christ's body is yourselves, each of you*
> *with a part to play in the whole.*

7. Discipline yourself to avoid returning to whatever caused the bondage. Satan will look for opportunities to win you back, but God will help you establish your new life, as is promised in 2 *Corinthians* 5:17 (NJB):

> *So for anyone who is in Christ, there is a new*
> *creation: the old order is gone and a new being*
> *is there to see.*

It takes effort to stride forward in the growth of holiness, but it is a marvelously rewarding path to follow. The farther we travel from our old ways, the easier it is to remain free of the past.

8. Pray the Lord's Prayer often, with meaning rather than by rote. It's a great deliverance prayer. It incorporates the essence of each of the first seven steps.

When needing deliverance, you can follow these steps on your own, but it's like trying to be your own doctor. You'll do much better if you work with someone who has experience in this. Jesus sent His disciples out two-by-two (*Mark* 6:7 NJB):

> *Then he summoned the Twelve and began to*
> *send them out in pairs, giving them authority*
> *over unclean spirits.*

A co-warrior who is not in bondage is freer than you to discern spirits, ignore their tactics and fight them off.

Arguing or trying to reason with demons is a mistake. Their intellects are superior to ours, and they're very crafty. You can't just talk them into leaving you alone. Not even Jesus conversed with them. He silenced them, rebuked them, and cast them out with a word.

Jesus had total authority over demons even before He won His victory on the cross. When the Holy Spirit became available to all believers on Pentecost, He gave us the same power. We can conquer demons with the simplicity of God's perfect strength. By commanding them in a voice that means business, we tell Satan that we know our authority comes from Christ.

People who help others (intercession) receive deliverance should first make sure they are ready and are called to it. It's not something we merely step into. Here's what's necessary:

- Know what you're doing. If you've never done this before, do it with someone else, and let them take the lead. Better yet, seek advice from a priest or deacon.
- Your life must be in submission to God; no unrepented sins. If you're still struggling to get out of the ruts of old bondages, wait until you are established in your new, healthy identity. Otherwise, you are likely to be messed with by the demons you're trying to cast out.
- Prayer and Scriptures should be a daily part of your life. Fasting is an added strength.
- Seek to glorify God, not yourself and your abilities to help somebody.
- Be motivated by love. This is very important! The amount of love you feel for the person you're helping is an indication of how filled up with God you are inside. Any lack of God (lack of love) leaves room for demons to interfere.
- Have a strong relationship with the Holy Spirit. You need to use His gifts.
- Wait until God tells you to do the deliverance prayers. You might not be the one He wants to use, or it might not be the right time yet. Rushing ahead of God could create an encounter with demons that should be avoided.
- Once the deliverance is planned, discern ahead of time what to pray for and what to expel.
- Before beginning the deliverance, repent of any sins or

unbelief in God's powers, relinquish trust in your own abilities, and ask God to do the work.

Desire to help is not enough. I know of a pastor who tried to help a young man, but the pastor's efforts had disastrous results. Gerard* had been a satanist for years. He had been involved in many aspects of the occult. The demons holding him in bondage were numerous and powerful.

A Christian friend gave him a gift she had secretly asked God to bless, thinking this might chase the demons away. She didn't tell Gerard that God had made it holy, but when she handed it to him, he recoiled from it and screamed. He refused to take it, even though the gift itself was something he wanted.

When the pastor of a local church came in to help, he sat in the living room with Gerard's mother to pray for him. The young man, elsewhere in the house, felt disturbed. He went to the living room and demanded that they stop praying. The pastor started telling him about Jesus. Gerard went berserk. Screaming and swearing, he threw furniture and smashed whatever was in his reach.

The well-meaning pastor did not know that his prayers for Jesus' help would anger the demons who were influencing Gerard. He did not know that binding Satan and the demons could have stopped the rampage. He did not know that casting them away from Gerard was necessary before there would even be a chance of the young man listening to him witness about Jesus. And he didn't realize that first Gerard had to agree to the deliverance. Demons won't let go if the person they're holding onto doesn't renounce them.

Anyone involved in spiritual warfare must learn what it takes to win. When healing or deliverance is asked for rightly, it comes every time (as God's will might so determine). The power of Christ's victory is that strong. If the prayers don't work, it's usually because the person is not willing to give up the bondage, or because the one praying has not sufficiently prepared for the ministry.

The Name of Jesus

Everyone who believes in Jesus and follows His ways can do the same things Jesus did. Jesus promised in *Mark* 16:17 (NJB):

> *These are the signs that will be associated with believers: in my name they will cast out devils .*

The name of Jesus represents all that Jesus is and the sacrifice He made for us on the cross. Using it should remind us of His nearness and His victory. Praying in His name indicates we have united our own will with God's — and that releases His power.

We cannot conquer the enemy by ourselves. We have to put Jesus in the center of our battles, and we accomplish that by calling on His name. St. Paul insisted on the importance of this in *Colossians* 3:17, when he said, "Whatever you say or do, let it be in the name of the Lord Jesus". If we did everything in Jesus' name (this also means by His will), we'd avoid many unnecessary battles, and when fighting demons, we'd be victorious.

The Power of Blessings

After I had been delivered of my occult background, I entered a new phase of warfare. Friends of mine were still involved in the occult. Was I to sit back and pray and wait for them to find the Lord? Or was I to preach to them whenever I had the chance? The answer to both was "no".

In spiritual warfare, we must stay on the offensive, rather than give Satan any opportunity to increase his hold on his victims. We pray and wait, and we use the time to show them that God cares by the way we care about them. We share our faith — gently — when God creates the opportunity, and we let them see God's power at work in us. St. Paul gave excellent advice on this in 2 *Timothy* 2:25, 26 (NJB):

> *He must be gentle when he corrects people who*
> *oppose him, in the hope that God may give them*
> *a change of mind so that they recognise the*
> *truth and come to their senses, escaping the trap*
> *of the devil who made them his captives and*
> *subjected them to his will.*

One of my friends, Denise*, lived with her friend, Stanley*, who taught her much about the occult. He was probably a satanist, for he had the paraphernalia for Black Masses in their apartment.

Denise, knowing of my previous interest in the occult, invited me to her weekly occult group. I wondered what kind of influence I could bring to the meeting. I knew that Jesus in me was stronger than Satan in the meeting, so I thought that maybe I could witness about the greater supernatural power I'd found in Jesus. Maybe I could convert someone.

I prayed about it and sought the counsel of a priest. He advised me not to go near the group.

He was right. The demons involved in their lives would not have allowed them to hear me and believe me, and their control over their victims was enhanced by the group setting.

Instead of going to the meeting, I asked the Lord to bless the people and be present to them. Guess what happened! For some reason, which no one in the group could figure out, everyone failed to get to the meeting that night. After that, the group disbanded!

When God blesses something, it becomes surrounded by His holiness, and demons cannot tolerate that. This is one reason why Jesus told us to bless our enemies.

Proof of the power of blessings is the way demon-possessed people respond to sacred objects. A report of a 1928 case tells of a forty-year-old possessed woman from Iowa who knew the difference between blessed and unblessed food. In an 1865 report, a rosary was placed near two young, demon-possessed German brothers, Theobald and Josef, while they slept. They cowered under their blankets until it was removed. Theobald even detected religious artifacts that had secretly been sewn into his clothes.

Another example comes from a spiritual battle I fought for Denise. I wanted Stanley's influence out of her life. Christmas was coming, so I bought two identical shirts as gifts. On the back of Denise's, I embroidered a picture of Stanley. On the back of Stan's, a picture of Denise. Ordinarily, they would have liked this.

Unknown to them, however, I prayed that each stitch would represent a prayer for God to bless their relationship. Denise and Stanley held these blessings in their hands on Christmas morning.

A week later, Stanley packed up and moved to the other side of the country. There had been no warning, no previous plans. But, suddenly, he could stay no longer.

The Help of Angels

Just as we can bind fallen angels and send them away, so too we can call upon holy angels and ask them to help us. (To prevent confusion, I'll keep referring to the fallen angels as demons. When I speak of angels, assume I mean the holy spirits. But keep in mind that when New Agers mention angels, they don't realize there are **evil** angels disguising themselves as good ones.)

"Spiritual forces and resources are available to all Christians," according to Rev. Billy Graham. "Because our resources are unlimited, Christians will be winners. Millions of angels are at God's command and at our service."[1] The Bible confirms this in *Hebrews* 1:14 when St. Paul admonishes, "Are [angels] not all ministering spirits, sent to serve for the sake of those who are to inherit salvation?"

An angel sat beside me as I wrote this book. Although he's protected me from demon interference and probably even told me when to move paragraphs and where to add something I hadn't thought of, I especially knew of his assistance when I deliberately asked for his help.

I couldn't find a certain scripture I wanted to include in the book. I had looked on Friday, perusing concordances, indexes and cross-references, but I'd failed. I went on with the writing. Monday, I searched again to no avail.

"Why am I getting frustrated?" I said. "I have an angel here to help me! Holy angel of God, in the name of Jesus Christ, show me where this verse is." I set the open Bible on my desk. "Go ahead and turn the page to it," I said. "Don't mind me if I freak out when I see the pages flip. Just find it!"

I thumbed through another book and then noticed my Bible's pages did not lie flat. There was a gap.

"Hmmm, I wonder—" I mused. I opened the Bible to that gap. There, in the middle of the page, I found the elusive verse.

A 1989 poll found that seventy-four percent of American teenagers believe that angels exist. A survey of Catholic college students revealed that more than eighty percent believe, and a 1994 poll showed that in the general population, seventy-two percent believe. Despite our great confidence in angels, however, we gravely under-use them. We give little thought to the invisible war they fight for us. But the Bible mentions in *Psalm* 91:10, 11 (NJB) how helpful angels really are:

> *No disaster can overtake you, no plague come*
> *near your tent; he has given his angels orders*
> *about you to guard you wherever you go.*

We should not try to hold conversations with angels, because demons often disguise themselves as "good" angels. But we can certainly expect them to help us in both simple and extraordinary ways. Irene Huber found that out, one night, when she was locking up the Marian

Center. She discovered that she had forgotten the key, and there was no one available with a spare. What was she going to do? She prayed.

A young man whom she had never seen before approached her and asked if she was trying to lock up the building. He had a key, so he locked it. When Irene turned to thank him, he was gone.

"No human being could have walked out of that parking lot that fast," she said later.

Why not ask angels to help you?

I did when Denise and Stanley and one of their friends told me they were coming to visit. They claimed they wanted to compare notes on what they believed about the occult with what I believed about Jesus. I suspected that their intentions were to convince me to return to my old interests.

Before they arrived, Ralph and I sprinkled the rooms of our house with holy water. We also prayed that God would post angels at every door and window to keep all evil spirits from entering.

When the threesome arrived, they planned to stay an hour. However, the subject of the occult never came up. They discussed the weather, our jobs, the house — anything but what they came to talk about. They sat nervously on the edge of the sofa. In less than fifteen minutes, they were gone.

Supernatural Warriors

God gives us supernatural gifts for many reasons. They bring us closer to Him, they improve our lives, they're exciting and fulfilling, and He gives them to us simply because He loves us. God wants to share Himself with us, hence He gives us gifts that reflect His nature — His love, His wisdom, His healing, etc.

Since we live on a battlefield, these gifts empower us to be supernatural warriors. Once Jesus frees us from our own bondage, it's time to fight to free others. We are called to action in *Ephesians* 5:8-16 (NAB):

> *There was a time you were darkness, but now you are light in the Lord. Well then, live as children of light. Light produces every kind of goodness and justice and truth. Be correct in your judgment of what pleases the Lord. Take no part in vain deeds done in darkness; rather, condemn them. It is shameful even to mention the things these people do in secret; but when such deeds are condemned they are seen in the light of day, and all that then appears is light. . . . Make the most of the present opportunity, for these are evil days.*

We must openly condemn the occult while showing love for those who are caught up in its deceptions. Christians are responsible for showing people that they can overcome the power of Satan. In *Acts* 26:17 and 18 (NJB), Jesus tells us, just as He told Paul, that He sends us to those who need deliverance, and that no matter how much demons try to stop us, they will lose if we have Christ:

> *I shall rescue you from the people and from the nations to whom I send you to open their eyes, so that they may turn from darkness to light, from the dominion of Satan to God.*

The responsibility starts with Christian leaders, those to whom the Body of Christ looks for guidance. It starts with seminary instructors who teach the clergy who will teach the Body. God holds them accountable for the ignorance of the people. Ignorance about the battle is no protection from the enemy, and many have been lost to the enemy because of lack of knowledge.

Countless numbers have been left on the battlefield blind and naked. The arrows of the enemy have claimed their victims because no one has shown them how to be victorious in Christ. No wonder so many Christians turn to the occult! No wonder the New Age movement is growing faster than are Christian churches!

Churches are failing to attract people away from the occult because: 1) its members are too apathetic to get involved; 2) many are afraid to get involved because it's controversial; 3) they think demons and the occult belong to eras long ago, so it's nothing to worry about now, and 4) people are simply ignorant about the need.

Church authorities need to take the responsibility of selecting, training and supervising its members for exorcisms and deliverance. Otherwise, the untrained people muddle through and sometimes do more harm than good, and many victims of demons spend the rest of their lives in misery.

Satan doesn't want Christians to fight with God's weapons. He doesn't want us to become supernatural warriors. He'll do anything, given the opportunity, to make us lazy, or fearful of controversy, or disbelieving of evil supernatural powers. He'll do anything to keep us unprepared for battle. Since he wants our evangelization efforts to be ineffective, he makes us doubt the power of God or doubt that we should speak to others about the occult.

Delivering others from Satan's grasp is easier than he's been convincing us to believe. After all, we have God's supernatural arsenal at our disposal! We're assured of this in 2 *Corinthians* 10:3, 4 (NJB):

> *For although we are human, it is not by human methods that we do battle. The weapons with which we do battle are not those of human nature, but they have power, in God's cause, to demolish fortresses.*

If we try to change people's ideas about the occult simply through intellectual arguments, telling them the errors of their ways, then, yes, freeing them from Satan will be difficult. We need to show them love while using the weapons of spiritual warfare. We need to demonstrate the greater supernatural power and love of God, just as St. Paul did 1 *Corinthians* 2:4-5, when he said: *"What I spoke and proclaimed was not meant to convince by philosophical argument, but to demonstrate the convincing power of the Spirit, so that your faith should depend not on human wisdom but on the power of God."*

People involved in the New Age movement are more open to discovering Jesus than we might imagine. They are, after all, seeking spiritual awakening. They have an emptiness inside them. When Jesus is presented as the Revealer of Love and the Prince of Powers, rather than an ineffective weakling or a wooden statue modeling an uncaring church, many hungrily grasp on to Him (especially after the demons influencing them have been bound and gagged).

New Age followers seek self-realization. If we present ourselves as sinners, too, on a journey toward perfection, we can bring them into an awareness of their need for being transformed by Christ. There is always hope. We can find encouragement in the words of Pope John Paul II, written in *The Splendor of Truth:* "No darkness of error or of sin can totally take away from man the light of God the Creator. In the depths of his heart there always remains a yearning for absolute truth and a thirst to attain full knowledge of it."

To guide people to Christ, we must show them Christ and His love. That's accomplished every time we do something good for them, i.e., something that proves we care. If they know that their needs are important to us, then they can believe that their needs are important to Jesus. This is how they begin to trust us and turn to us with questions about their spiritual needs. Most of them will be more willing to listen if we focus on how much will be more willing to listen if we focus on how much Jesus loves them rather than on why the occult is sinful.

The key to victory is praying for them. We can break Satan's hold by silencing the forces that have been drowning out the love message of Christ. We can ask the Holy Spirit to open their ears to hear us and their eyes to see His love revealed through us. We should pray, also, for the timing of our evangelization efforts, for if we rush ahead of God we could act before they're ready.

The guiding rule is: Love them first. Then, if what you say will make a difference, say it. If it won't help, don't waste your time. With your advance prayers and the Holy Spirit alive within you, and with the love of the Father touching them through you, there will come a time when you *can* make a difference.

God has a New Age movement, too. It's His Kingdom coming to Earth, which began when the Messiah was first prophesied and which will reach completion when Christ triumphantly destroys all evil at His second coming. God's supernatural power is available to all the inhabitants of that Kingdom.

---

* Not their real names

---

[1] Billy Graham, *Angels: God's Secret Agents,* Carmel, NY: Guideposts Associates, Inc., 1975, p. 15.

Chapter 12

Living in the Fullness of God's Power

Every gift or power that comes from the occult is actually a counterfeit of God's greater gifts and powers.

Occult gifts come from spiritual forces that want to occult the Light of Christ. They are designed to lead us into the world of darkness. God's gifts, on the other hand, come from the Light of Christ and lead us into the Light of Truth. And what the Light reveals is love: divine love, supernatural love, unconditional love, true love, always love. The spiritual forces of the occult cannot even come close to imitating this gift from God. They offer what feels like love, but it's only lust, or empty promises, or a briefly lasting hope for satisfaction. ·

God is bigger, mightier, and much more loving than any power or spirit in the occult. He is bigger and mightier than any problem, need, hurt, or impossible situation we face. There is no greater supernatural gift than to know the love of the Creator of the universe. To those who make this the focus of their lives, He gives joy that lingers even in the midst of frustrations. He gives peace that lasts even through turmoil. In human experience, this is difficult to understand and impossible to achieve, but through the supernatural power of God, it is ours.

Experiencing God's love is achieved by growing in the holiness that you, as a baptized Christian, already have. "All are called to become a glorious church, holy and without blemish," said Pope John Paul II on February 2, 1994, in his *Letter to Families* for the International Year of the Family. "'Be holy,' says the Lord, 'for I am holy' (*Leviticus* 11:44). This is the deepest significance of the great mystery" of God's love, "a love which continually expands and lavishes on people an ever greater sharing in the supernatural life."

Jesus' life is a perfect example of the kind of supernatural powers available to us. Keep in mind that the motive behind His use of each supernatural gift was love — always love.

Jesus could **read people's minds**, that is, He had the gift of the word of knowledge (*John* 4:17, 18; *Luke* 5:22; *Matt.* 9:4) and since God knows the thoughts of all people, He can tell us, too, what someone is thinking. He empowers us with this knowledge to help us minister to others, understand their needs, or become united with them through love.

Jesus **foretold the future** (*John* 1:47, 48; *Luke* 19:28-34; Matt. 16:21). God's gift of prophecy is always accurate, unlike fortune telling. By giving us glimpses of the future (my family calls them "future-flashes") God encourages us, offers us hope, and gives us guidance. He does not use this gift to frighten us; therefore we can be sure that predictions are *not* from Him if they cause Christians to fear or hold us back from loving others.

Jesus **healed supernaturally**, but not the way psychic healers do. He did not use auras or pyramids or crystals. He did not prescribe remedies dictated by a spirit's voice as Edgar Cayce did. Nor did He pull out strands of foul-smelling flesh or materialize diseased organs through the skin as some occult healers do. Jesus simply healed by word and touch. We, too, can lay hands on people to allow the healing power of God to make a difference in their lives. Not everyone has a ministry of healing — because it's too easy to put the focus on ourselves and get caught up in the glamor and fame it brings — but every Christian does have a *gift* of healing in that we use it whenever we distribute God's love through prayers for healing, through showing that we care, and by listening to and addressing the hurts of other people.

Jesus **heard disembodied voices**, but it was always the

Father or angels to whom He listened (*John* 12:28-30). He knew the difference between theirs and Satan's voices. It's essential that we learn this, too. Although God does speak audibly sometimes, we need to train our hearts to recognize what He is telling us in silence, for He speaks to us all the time, guiding us, reassuring us, and helping us through all situations.

Jesus **talked to "ghosts"** during the Transfiguration on the mountain (*Luke* 9:28-36), but this was no seance. And Jesus never told His disciples to repeat this kind of event. It was a singularly unique encounter. Moses and Elijah cannot even really be called ghosts. They appeared to Jesus in glorified bodies, that is, physical bodies like those every believer will receive because of the second coming of Christ. Moses and Elijah met with Jesus as the highest representatives of the law and the prophets, the two main ways God revealed Himself before Jesus was born. Moses and Elijah were passing on their ministries to Jesus so He could bring them to the ultimate fulfillment.

Jesus **gained knowledge supernaturally** (*John* 7:15, 16; *Luke* 2:46, 47). He learned from the Holy Spirit, not through divination or channeling. Likewise, if we need to know, for example, that a friend is in trouble and needs our help, or that the job we're thinking of taking isn't right, the Holy Spirit does tell us.

Jesus levitated. How else could He have walked on water (*John* 6:19)? He **traveled supernaturally** (*John* 6:22-25). He **disappeared** when people tried to kill Him (*John* 8:59; 10:39). In everyday life, we have no need for these types of events to happen, but if we follow Jesus into a very challenging ministry, it can happen to us, too, if it glorifies God through the good He's called us to do.

Jesus had **power over animals** (*Luke* 5:4-7; *Matt.* 21:18, 19). If the need exists and we've matured spiritually enough to use this gift only for advancing God's kingdom, anything is possible through Him.

Jesus **transformed a little into a lot** (*Luke* 9:14-17) and

water **into wine** (*John* 2:7-10). He even miraculously
produced money when He needed it! (See *Matt.* 17:27.)
The multiplication of something out of next-to-nothing
happens today much more frequently than we realize,
usually when Christian organizations take care of other
people's needs.

Jesus **brought the dead back to life** (*Luke* 7:14, 15; 8:50;
John 11:43, 44). He **controlled clouds and wind and rain**
(*Luke* 8:24).

Whatever God the Father could do—countless amazing miracles throughout the Old Testament—Jesus could
do. Likewise, when we are filled with God's Spirit, we can
do it, too. Jesus promised in *John* 14:12 (NJB):

> *In all truth I tell you, whoever believes in me*
> *will perform the same works as I do myself, and*
> *will perform even greater works, because I am*
> *going to the Father.*

What were the "same works" Jesus did? What are the
"even greater works?" Putting this verse into context and
reading all of chapter fourteen, we can understand what
Jesus meant. The "same works" were those He did as a
man—a human like you and me. They were works of love,
like you and I can (and do) accomplish in our normal,
every day lives. The "greater works" are the supernatural
ones, because the Father makes them happen through us
when He calls us to special ministries.

God has provided ample evidence that His supernatural powers and gifts truly are available to us. The
book of *Acts* tells story after story of Christians performing
supernatural wonders in the name of Jesus. The lives of
Saints also show that anything's possible. For example:

The face of St. Sebastian, a young Roman officer,
glowed supernaturally when he told people about the
Lord. St. Lucy, around A.D. 304, refused to budge from
her beliefs—literally! Soldiers, pagan magicians, and even
a team of oxen could not move her from the spot where

she prayed. When they tried to burn her, the flames were held back by unseen forces.

St. Patrick knew when a distant ship would be available to help him escape slavery—an angel told him in a dream, while St. Brigid's butter and milk multiplied as she gave it away to the poor. God also gave her milk from depleted cows and fruit from trees that had been picked clean.

St. Columban freed Christian prisoners by having their iron chains shatter from a touch. When these prisoners sought refuge in a church, Columban commanded the locked doors to open, then slam shut to keep out those who had chased them. Not even the sexton's keys could reopen them.

Wild animals obeyed St. Francis of Assisi, including a wolf that had been killing people and cattle and St. Clare of Assisi, when her convent was being invaded by a horde of Mohammedans, showed them the consecrated Host in its monstrance. The enemy fled. When she was too ill to attend Christmas Eve Mass, she saw and heard the full service in a vision.

St. Catherine of Sienna, at the age of seven, wandered too far from home. An invisible force levitated her and sped her back. As an adult, she kneaded spoiled dough and watched it miraculously freshen. And when interrogated by bishops who challenged her intelligence, she came up with all the right answers despite a lack of education.

St. Bernardine of Sienna restored to life a young man who had been killed by a bull and St. Frances of Rome, needing grain for the poor, prayed before an empty bin. It filled in seconds! When the enemy captured her little son, none of the horses they put him on would budge until he was returned to his mother.

St. Philip Neri foresaw that the ship a friend was going to travel on would be ambushed by Turks. When it happened, the friend started to drown and called out, "Father, save me!" Philip appeared and carried him across the water to safety. Philip often levitated when he celebrated Mass. St. Frances Xavier Cabrini, the first U.S. citizen to be canonized a Saint, needed to dig a well for a new orphanage and novitiate house. Rather than using the occult method of dowsing, she asked God to show her where to dig. They found water on the first try.

In modern times, Padre Pio, not yet canonized a Saint, appeared to people who needed help, although his body was still back home. However, unlike the occult counterfeit of astral projection, he was seen in a touchable body, sometimes in several places at once around the world.

There is much, much more of the supernatural in the lives of Saints, but they did not consider such power surprising. Their source, after all, was God. They took seriously *Philippians* 4:13 which states, "There is nothing I cannot do in the One who strengthens me".

This is the way Christ intended all of us to live. After His resurrection, just before He ascended into heaven, He said (*Acts* 1:8 NJB): *"You will receive the power of the Holy Spirit."*

When we are filled with the Spirit of God, supernatural powers become natural. So why don't we see more use of these powers today? It's not because people don't believe in miracles. Forty-seven percent of Americans completely agree with this statement: "Even today, miracles are performed by the power of God." Thirty-five percent mostly agree. Only four percent completely disagree.[1]

The reasons we don't see more miracles today are because we don't want to spend the time and effort to grow spiritually, and so we excuse our lack of supernatural powers by assuming it's not meant for us and not available now. Finally we don't always trust God's ways of solving problems, or trust His timing.

Miracles don't happen without God, yet He's not the center of our lives. We do much every day without Him.

let too much distract us from putting Him first.

A large part of the problem is the times we live in. We're used to getting everything fast and easy. Microwave ovens, jet airplanes, push-button telephones, computers, fax machines, and medicines that speed healings: these time-saving inventions are a blessing to our physical lives, but a curse to our spiritual lives. They've created a generation of "give-it-to-me-now" spoiled brats. We've lost the patience to wait for God's perfect timing. (Our idea of perfect timing is not God's!)

It takes years to develop blind trust in God, years to grow in the love for others through which God channels His power. We mature in holiness only gradually. Even though we can experience a taste of God's power right now, just the way we are, we want more fast. We're not used to waiting, so we turn away from God and resort to shortcuts. It's a big reason the occult is so popular.

Another curse is the comfort all our modern conveniences provide. Daily life is filled with pleasures, even when we're miserable. The furnaces and thermostats, plumbing and water heaters, telephones and ambulances we take for granted have become our false gods. We rely on them first, then maybe turn to God if all else fails. When our car breaks down in the middle of nowhere, don't we hike to a phone to call a tow truck before we think of praying? When the flu strikes our family, don't we run to the doctor or the medicine cabinet faster than we run to God? We should first ask God for help, then use the towing service or doctor He guides us to—but don't be surprised if the miraculous happens.

When our daughter, Tammy, was six months old, her stomach didn't develop properly. She could not keep her food down. Repeated trips to the pediatrician accomplished nothing but increased worry. We'd forgotten to turn to God. When the doctor said we'd have to put her into a children's hospital, Ralph and I finally decided to call the prayer chain at church. That night was the last time

Tammy threw up.

With all the speed and comfort our society provides, we forget to seek the Giver of Miracles. St. Leo the Great saw this danger from the fifth century: "Even the things that are necessary for human existence can be a snare to us, absorbing our energy and spiritual vigor to the neglect of the things of God."[2]

Put God First

Step one toward holy supernatural power is training ourselves to think of God first—in all things—and then trust Him for perfect timing. Remember, God knows more about what's best for us than we do. And He wants what's best for us more than we do. Jesus told us we should never worry because our heavenly Father understands what we need. But for His help to reach us we must follow the advice He gives in *Matthew* 6:33 (NJB):

> *Set your hearts on his kingdom first, and on God's saving justice, and all these other things will be given you as well.*

First Corinthians 4:20 tells us that the Kingdom of God is power. Jesus' central message was "Repent, for the Kingdom of God is at hand." He was inviting us to receive power that could only come through a change from worldly ways to God's ways, from self-centeredness to unconditional love. The more we turn away from the "gifts" and "gods" of the world to fix our minds on God's Kingdom, the more His greater supernatural power and love can work in us.

God should be more important to us than our problems. Jesus did not say, "Call on me only when you can't solve the problem yourself." He told us to always put God first. Then we can trust Him to guide our efforts to work out the problem. And we can trust that when our efforts alone aren't enough, God will do the rest.

When we don't seek God's help, we tend to give

ourselves credit for the work that's accomplished. But we cannot grow strong in faith if we glorify ourselves for what we do. We need to see God's power at work. Failing to put God first in our lives is the sin of pride—the same sin that felled Satan. When we need to rely on God, but choose instead to rely solely on ourselves or someone or something else, we are saying that God is less loving and less powerful than the person or thing we are turning to. We all do it, but how wrong we are!

The Power of the Holy Spirit

There is nothing more loving and more powerful than God. It was Jesus who actually told us we "receive power when the Holy Spirit has come upon you" (*Acts* 1:8). We have all had those times when we respond to problems with a nauseating wave of fear instead of trusting God. But St. Paul told us in 2 *Timothy* 1:7 (NJB):

> *God did not give you a Spirit of timidity, but the Spirit of power.*

The more we are filled with His Spirit, the more we experience His power. But the more we are absorbed in ourselves and the lies of Satan, the more we let fear clog up that power.

I can see this in my own life. One day, I visited a friend after a shopping trip. I hadn't thought much about the Lord that morning, so I felt very much affected by the atmosphere in the stores. Comparing prices, looking for bargains, failing to find the right pajamas for my son, and coping with unfriendly customers left me tense and self-absorbed. I didn't even want to listen to the Christian music tape I usually played in the car.

When I arrived at my friend's house, I found her son home from school with the flu. Should I pray for him, I wondered? What if my prayers didn't work? Then I'd look like a fool. Can I risk failing? My thoughts focused on me instead of God. I couldn't even bring myself to ask my friend if she'd like me to pray. Afterward, I kept berating myself for failing to give God this moment to use me to show His love.

By contrast, the next morning I started the day out right. I asked God to forgive me for being too filled with myself before. I thanked Him for the new day and asked Him to take charge of it. I read my Bible. And when I left home to attend a luncheon, I kept Him in my thoughts.

The woman I sat next to (a coincidence? I think not!) — unknown to me — had been wondering if God still performs miracles of healing. After the program, we began to chat. I sensed God telling me to ask her if one of her legs was shorter than the other.

If this had happened the day before, I would have thought, "No way! I'll sound ridiculous!" But today I could obey. Sure enough, one leg was shorter.

"Do you want to see a miracle?" I asked, filled with excitement. She sat down; I held her feet and began to command the short leg to grow out in the name of Jesus. About a minute later, the legs were even.

God's power flows through us when we stay near to Him, through daily prayer time, reading the Bible, listening to Christian music, attending Christ-centered seminars and prayer meetings and retreats, frequent use of the Sacraments, reading books about God and Saints, worshipping Him with community, etc. The more time we spend with Him, the more we experience His supernatural power and love.

The Power of Renewal

We were all made in the image of God, but that image needs continual rebirth. As St. Leo said:

> We were meant to be like a mirror reflecting
> his likeness in all its beauty and goodness.
> We know only too well, however, that this
> reflection is obscured and tarnished by all

kinds of obstacles within ourselves. The nature we inherited from Adam is a wounded and fallen one, and unless it is healed and raised up again by Christ, the second Adam, there is nothing we can do of ourselves to become what we are meant to be.[3]

It is the Holy Spirit who transforms us into that reflection of God's power, but only if we are willing. He removes our wrong aims and unloving attitudes so we can be more wholly focused on Christ's Kingdom. He removes all the obstacles within us that impede His power. He teaches us everything we need to know about who God really is, how powerful He is, and what He has promised us.

He does not do this alone. We have to commit ourselves to this transformation. It takes time and effort to get to the place where St. Paul can say of us (2 *Cor.* 12:12 NJB):

> *All the marks characteristic of a true apostle have been at work among you: complete perseverance, signs, marvels, demonstrations of power.*

The Power of Prayer

Prayer brings us into the holy presence of God. It's impossible to experience God's power without it. St. Paul learned this from experience and he advised us to "keep praying in the Spirit on every occasion" (*Ephesians* 6:18). Pray in the Spirit, that is, in unity with the will of God. Pray on every possible occasion. To pray constantly is to keep God in our minds on some level, all through the day, every day. It's letting Him interpret the events of our day, staying tuned in to His guidance, doing our work in a way that will please Him, and running all our decisions by Him first, from the least to the largest. Prayer should become a habit for He is the most important thing in the universe; without Him, nothing would exist. Yet how often we ignore Him!

There's a story about four men, all but one living in troubled marriages. Each was asked how much time he spent talking to his wife. One said, "Twice a year, on Easter and Christmas." Another said, "About once a month, whenever I've got nothing better to do." A third said, "Once a week, on Sundays." But the fourth said, "Every day. I make time to talk to her in the morning before I get out of bed, and she's the last person I talk to at night. And any other chance I get, I give her a call."

How often do you talk to your heavenly Spouse? The more time you spend communicating with God, the more you will see His power in your life.

The Power of Faith

Faith, we are told by the *Sacred Congregation for the Doctrine of the Faith,* can "give us confidence, by assuring us that the power of Satan cannot go beyond the limits set by God. . . . Above all, faith opens the heart to prayer, in which it finds its victory and its crown. It thus enables us to triumph over evil through the power of God."

Jesus told us that if we have faith and no doubts, we can move mountains (*Mark* 11:22-24). Have you moved any mountains lately? A mountain could be a severe illness, the loss of a job, or any major problem.

How difficult it is to have no doubts! And yet, faith is not something we can conjure up by our own power. Faith is a gift from the Holy Spirit (see 1 *Cor.* 12:9). United with Him, we have within us all the faith that He has! The key to overcoming our doubts is trusting God. When I pray, "Jesus, you be my trust, help my unbelief," I see better results than when I rely solely on my own efforts.

God can perform miracles without us. He can answer our prayers before we even turn to Him. But most of the time He prefers to work *through* us. That allows our free will to play a part. We can choose to rely on Him or we can choose to ignore Him.

When we ask for a miracle, or when we lift up our prayers to God, we need to open ourselves to receive His help. Receiving His help takes trust. Trust takes time. The more we let God work, the quicker our trust grows. We're told in *Hebrews* 12:2 (NJB):

> *Let us keep our eyes fixed on Jesus, who leads us*
> *in our faith and brings it to perfection.*

Of course it becomes easier to trust God when we understand what God's will is concerning our problem. We learn His will through prayer, through the Bible, through others who are close to God, and by looking for evidence of His activity. For example, if you're confused about what kind of job you should pursue, pray about it, find scriptures that deal with it, talk to other Christians who know where your talents lay, and look for "doors" (job opportunities) that God may be opening or closing.

When we pray **according** to God's will, the gift of faith He's given us becomes active. But when we reject Him, such as by insisting we get things exactly the way we want them when we want them, we frustrate ourselves and our patience. God wants only what's best for us. If we find no peace in following God's will, it's because we don't completely trust Him.

Trust is a muscle. It has to be exercised to grow strong. Trust is hope turned into action. It becomes a powerful force when we make sure our request is within God's will and then act on our prayers as if they're already answered, because that shows our complete trust in God.

For example, I mentioned in an earlier chapter that my husband and I wanted to go to a Christian conference but couldn't find someone to watch our young kids. Believing that the Lord wanted us to go, I started making plans. I knew that God often waits for the last minute to answer prayers to test our trust and patience, so I refused to worry as the conference weekend approached. Sure enough, Thursday night a friend offered to take the kids.

Jesus had promised He would help me—and all of us—in *Mark* 11:24 (NJB):

> *I tell you, therefore, everything you ask and pray for, believe that you have it already, and it will be yours.*

The Power of Words

Our spoken words have far more power than we imagine. They spread like ripples on a pond, effecting changes we cannot perceive. We hurt others with careless words. We blaspheme God and our own spirits with curses. We bring sickness on through self-fulfilling prophecies ("I always get the flu in January.")

Words have more power to make ripples than do our thoughts. The Bible doesn't tell us to wish for the power of the Holy Spirit; it tells us to ask for it (*Matt.* 7:7 NJB).

When we ask for a miracle—for example, a better job—we should request it out loud in the name (i.e., the *will*) of Jesus. I asked God, one day, why I sometimes doubted He would answer my prayers. I had usually prayed silently. Suddenly it occurred to me that when I prayed silently, God seemed to me to be no bigger than my own mind. When I prayed out loud, I realized I was praying to a God who is bigger than the universe. That increased my ability to trust Him.

Praying out loud can also set the spirit world in action. Demons cannot read our minds if Christ dwells within us. Therefore, they have to hear us *speak* the power of God. For example, they have to hear that our job search is off limits to their interference.

Speaking our prayers also activates our faith. Even secular books on how to be successful tell us to speak our desires. Psychologists say that if we want to change a habit or reach a goal, announcing that we're accomplishing it actually helps us to achieve it. It empowers us to believe in the goal and in our ability to effect the change.

Another way to speak our prayers is to pray the Word of God. Find scripture verses that relate to your situation and read them aloud. For example, when I have a speaking engagement, I might pray *John* 10:2-3, beforehand: "Dear Lord, you be the Shepherd of the flock that is here today. Help me be the gatekeeper that lets you in. Let these sheep hear your voice."

We can also quote Scriptures the way Jesus did when Satan tempted Him in the desert. You could say, "It is written that Jesus gave Himself for my sins to rescue me from this present evil (*Gal.* 1:4), so the demons at work against me now must stop!"

Our words can destroy, thus giving Satan opportunities to work, or they can unite us with God, empowering us to see miracles.

The Power of Praise

Some of the most powerful words are those that praise and glorify God. God *commands* us to praise Him in 1 *Thessalonians* 5:16-18 (NJB):

> *Always be joyful; pray constantly; and for all things give thanks; this is the will of God for you in Christ Jesus.*

God does not insist on this because it strokes His ego, but because praise increases our trust. Every day, we have reasons to praise God. When He answers prayer, we should praise Him. Better yet, when we ask for His help, we should show our trust by thanking Him before His answer comes. But most important, in the midst of problems we should praise God despite our feelings, because then we're placing our trust in God's love above the evidence of trouble. This sacrifice of praise is powerful, as shown in *Psalm* 8:1, 2 (NJB):

> *Yahweh our Lord, how majestic is your name*

throughout the world! Whoever keeps singing of
your majesty higher than the heavens . . . you
make him a fortress, firm against your foes, to
subdue the enemy and the rebel.

The teenage son of a friend of mine was hit by a truck. As his mother cradled his broken skull in her hands, covering his exposed brains, she praised God through her tears. She said, "Thank you Jesus for helping my son. Thank you Jesus, thank you Jesus."

Then a soothing voice seemed to say, "This is not unto death. This is for My glory." It filled her with peace and reassurance. Her praises increased.

At the hospital, miracle followed miracle. His smashed cheek bones knit together in one day! The boy recovered with only a few scars and a metal plate in his head as proof the accident had really happened.

God cares for us more than we can hope for. When we focus on this, rather than on how bad the problem looks, praise becomes easy. Praising God means we know the meaning of 2 *Corinthians* 4:7 (NJB): *"The immensity of the power is God's and not our own."*

The Power of Fellowship

Christian fellowship is essential. There is power in numbers. It is often easier for people to get miraculous healings in a large healing service than in their own, private prayer time?

Christian community provides growth, encouragement, support, instruction, and greater exposure to God's spiritual gifts. When we're weak and discouraged, we can turn to the joy and confidence of those who are walking in God's power. The more we're surrounded by people who are strong in the Lord, the more we become aware of the Lord's presence. Jesus promised in *Matthew* 18:19, 20 (NJB):

In truth I tell you once again, if two of you on

> *earth agree to ask anything at all, it will be
> granted to you by my Father in heaven. For
> where two or three meet in my name, I am there
> among them.*

"God is working in a special and unique way in and through the Christian community," Dr. John Newport has said concerning the way God's power breaks into our world. "The church's mission is to witness to the Kingdom in the world and to be the instrument of the Kingdom."[4]

The Holy Spirit empowers community members to build each other up in trust and love. Pope John Paul II made mention of this in a homily on October 30, 1987:

> [Individuals] can never remain in isolation
> from the community, but must live in a
> continual interaction with others, with a
> lively sense of fellowship, rejoicing in an
> equal dignity and common commitment to
> bring to fruition the immense treasure that
> each has inherited. . . . Thus the charisms,
> the ministries, the different forms of service
> exercised by the lay faithful exist in
> communion and on behalf of communion.
> They are treasures that complement one
> another for the good of all and are under
> the wise guidance of their Pastors.

In Conclusion

Much of our powerlessness comes from trying to do God's part, i.e., trying to handle problems without seeking God. And it comes from expecting God to do it without us. We cannot sit back and wait for everything to fall into our laps. God and you make a team. If you work together, you always win.

God wants us to use His power. He gave it to us at the cost of His Son's life. Jesus suffered the most brutal death in order to release the fullness of God's power in our lives.

Our lives. Are we going to deny that? Reject it? Ignore it? Or act upon it?

God has a divine response to the New Age movement: bigger and better supernatural power, combined with ultimate truth and pure love. As people search for supernatural power, if we say "yes" to God's invitation to be His witnesses, He will work through us to show them where they can find the greatest and the best.

Are you willing to become a channel of His love?

Let us join together in praying *Ephesians* 3:20:

> **Glory be to him whose power, working in us, can do infinitely more than we can ask or imagine!**

---

[1] According to the Princeton Religion Research Center, 1989.

[2] Anne Field, *The Binding of the Strong Man*, Ann Arbor, MI: Word of Life, 1976, pp. 58, 59.

[3] Ibid., p. 23.

[4] Dr. John Newport, *The Biblical and Occult Worlds — A 20th Century Confrontation* tape series, Fort Worth, TX: Latimer House Publishing Co., 1973, "The Christian Alternative to Magic: The Kingdom of God."

Appendix A

Prayers for Help

Prayer for the Presence of Christ

Lord Jesus, I know I have sinned against You. Forgive me. I want the love that You offer. I want to become the kind of person God the Father created me to be. I want You to be my Friend, my Guide, my Savior. I want You to be in charge of my life and empower me with Your Holy Spirit. Fill me with Your presence, Your love, Your peace. I thank You for dying on the cross for me. Thank You for loving me even though I haven't loved You as I should. Lord, I believe in You; help my unbelief.

Prayer for the Power of the Holy Spirit

Come, Holy Spirit, and renew me so that I can reach my fullest potential. Fill me to overflowing with Your gifts, Your power, Your love. I open myself to receive all that the Father has for me. He is the Creator of everything and, through Christ, He has made me His adopted child. Therefore far more is available to me than I ever imagined. Help me to receive it all. Teach me how to use Your gifts. Instruct me in all truth. Fill my mind with Your thoughts and help me to recognize Your voice. Make me an instrument of the Father's will.

Prayer to Conquer Evil

Satan, in the name of Jesus Christ, I bind you from interfering in this [you name it] situation in any way. You have no right to interfere with [whatever problem is occurring] because I [or the person you're praying for] am a child of God Almighty! So, in the name of Jesus Christ, I cast you out of this situation now and command you not to return. Go now to the foot of the cross!

Then pray:

You spirit of [name the problem], in the name of Jesus Christ, I bind you and I cast you away from this situation, now, and I command you never to return! And don't send any other evil spirits back to me, and do not retaliate in any way.

After doing this for every spirit
the Holy Spirit brings to your mind, pray:

Father, in the name of Your Son, Jesus Christ, resolve this situation according to Your will and Your love. I leave it in Your hands and refuse to worry about it any more. Jesus, fill me [or the person you're praying for] with Your presence, Your love, Your peace, Your joy, and [the opposite of everything that was cast away]. Holy Spirit, fill me [or that person] with Your power and Your gifts. Father, surround [who] with holy angels to protect me/them and fight off the attacks of demons. Bless [the person or situation] and replace all the evil with Your holiness. Jesus, pour Your precious blood over [who] and my/their home, friendships, workplace, activities, etc. Thank You, Father, Son and Holy Spirit! I praise You and worship You for what You are doing, how You are doing it, and when You've chosen as the best time for finishing it. Amen!

Appendix B

New Age or God: Which Offers More Power?

God tells us to test everything rather than blindly believing whatever we learn (1 *Thess.* 5:21, 22). We are to judge teachings of the New Age movement by their fruits (*Matt.* 7:16, 17). The most important fruits are where it leads us: closer to Jesus Christ or away from Him. Does a New Age belief contradict the Gospel message of salvation or does it help us to live holier lives? Note how New Age concepts differ from truth on the following topics.

Who is God?

New Age: God is a transcendent, impersonal force, neither good nor evil. He (sometimes called She or It) is a cosmic consciousness of which we are all a part. Therefore everything is divine. By extension, that means even perverse acts are accepted; anything is permissible.

Christianity: God is three-in-one Trinity of Father, Son and Holy Spirit. He alone is divine. He is not only transcendent, but He is also personally and intimately involved in our lives because He cares about each of us. He is perfect goodness and love. He knows our thoughts. He wants good things to happen to us. The more we get to know Him and live the way He tells us to, the more we will experience His supernatural love and power in our lives.

> *Yahweh, what quantities of good things you have in store for those who fear you, and bestow on those who make you their refuge, for all humanity to see (Psalm 31:19 NJB).*

Who is Jesus?

New Age: Jesus was one of many enlightened masters who achieved a high level of spirituality. He can help us find our own divinity. Some believe He was a spirit-being from outer space.

Christianity: Jesus is God's only divine Son. He was both man and God, born miraculously without the sperm-seed of a human father. He sacrificed Himself for us, taking our sins upon Himself on the cross. Then He rose from the dead. We receive *His* divinity when we are baptized and when we make Him the Lord of our lives. He leads us to a personal relationship with God our Father.

> *The Father sent his Son as Saviour of the world. Anyone who acknowledges that Jesus is the Son of God, God remains in him and he in God* (1 John 4:14, 15 NJB).

What is Creation?

New Age: All is one; everything is interrelated, including the cosmos, the spirit world, humanity, God, and nature. All the world's problems result from not recognizing this unity, rather than from the existence of evil.

Christianity: God created diversity. God is not one with His creation, but superior to it. Therefore we are not equal to God. Likewise, we are not one with nature; He made us masters over it. Problems result from disobeying God and failing to turn to Him for help in a world that is infiltrated by Satan and his minions.

> *God created the heavens and the earth. . . Male and female he created . . . God said to them . . . have dominion over the fish of the sea and over the birds of the air and over every living thing* (Gen.1:1, 27, 28 RSV).

Humankind

New Age: We are immortal. We are all God. If we discover The Christ (the divine) within us, we can heal ourselves and use other supernatural powers.

Christianity: If we were God, we'd be omniscient, omnipotent and omnipresent, but we are not. We are God's creation. He made us in His image; therefore we reflect His goodness and love. However, because we sin, we separate ourselves from God and reflect evil. This separation robs us of the spiritual gifts God intends to share with us, including supreme love now and a joy-filled eternal life in Heaven later.

> *All men have sinned and are deprived of the glory of God (Rom. 3:23 NAB).*

What is Salvation?

New Age: Salvation is discovering your higher or divine self. There is life after death for all, with no punishment for the wicked. Reincarnation is one way people reach perfection. In other words, we save ourselves.

Christianity: Since we are all sinners, we cannot save ourselves from eternal death. However, if we trust in Jesus, who took our sins to the cross, and repent from sinful ways, we will receive forgiveness. Then we benefit from *His* supernatural power. We receive His love and forgiveness and healing from death. Only then can we have eternal joy in Heaven.

> *Jesus the Messiah. . . There is salvation in no one else! . . . there is no other name for men to call upon to save them (Acts 4:11, 12 TLB).*

Supernatural Power

New Age: Crystals harmonize mental, physical and spiritual energies. Colors can heal. Charms ward off evil. Spirits or beings from other dimensions or other planets work miracles and predict the future. Pyramids collect power. Magic is within your mind.

Christianity: All the powers of the occult are counterfeits of God's greater gifts, and they ultimately lead us away from Him. Some are fake, all are misleading. Crystals are simply beautiful rocks created by God. Charms are worthless; if they have any power, it comes from demons. We need not fear evil if Jesus is our Lord, for He has overcome the power of Satan when He sacrificed Himself on the cross and rose again to life. The only supernatural source that benefits us completely and lastingly, and that helps us spiritually, emotionally and physically, is the power that comes to us through Jesus Christ, who said:

> *Whoever believes in me will perform the same works as I do myself, and will perform even greater works (John 14:12).*

Will There Be a New World?

New Age: The world is in bad shape and will soon be saved by a new, universal religion where everything is one. Some say this will happen because we will evolve into a united higher consciousness. This is known as the Quantum Leap. Others say "space brothers" from another planet will rescue us. In the past, many said that the new world would be ushered in by the astrological Age of Aquarius that dawned in the 1960s, or the Harmonic Convergence held on August 16-17, 1987.

Christianity: There is a new world coming, even better than the one imagined by New Agers, but it will arrive when Jesus Christ returns in power and glory to judge the world, destroy all evil, and create a new Heaven and new earth. We cannot predict when this will occur, because only Our Father knows the time.

> *I saw a new heaven and a new earth . . . God himself will be with them . . . death shall be no more, neither shall there be mourning nor crying nor pain (Rev. 21:1, 3, 4 RSV).*

Appendix C

Danger Signs

The following are "caution flags" that might indicate someone is involved in the occult. The more signs you see, the greater should be your concern.

1. Books on the occult, fiction and non-fiction.
2. Artwork or doodling of occult or satanic symbols, often found on clothing, notebooks, tattoos, territorial markings, etc.
3. A fascination with horror movies or novels.
4. Spending time in meditation and chanting without Jesus.
5. A new vocabulary, using occult terms.
6. Playing with *Dungeons and Dragons, The Gathering,* Ouija boards, Tarot cards and other occult "games," having seances, consulting fortune tellers, etc.
7. An unusual arrangement of crystals, candles, good luck charms, chalices, and other occult paraphernalia.
8. Interest in the posters, T-shirts and music of rock groups that use occult symbols or refer to Satan, especially heavy or black metal bands.
9. Wearing silver jewelry (gold is considered the color of Christianity) with satanic symbols, charms, etc.
10. Wearing all black clothing, fingernails, eye makeup, etc. Another favorite color is blood red.
11. Messages with everything written backwards.
12. Photographs or videos of death and gore.
13. A *Book of Shadows,* usually a black notebook for the person's own spells, dark poetry, artwork, pledges to Satan, demons, prior and intended victims, etc.
14. The *Satanic Bible,* the *Satanic Ritual* or other books with witchcraft or satanic themes.

15. Moodier, lower self-esteem, depression.

16. Withdrawal from old friends, hanging out with a small clique of new friends.

17. Abrupt change in attitude or behavior for the worse, especially with aggression, hatred for authority and law enforcement, alienation from family, school (or work) performance.

18. Increased secretiveness regarding the bedroom, locking the door; evasive about activities, friends and interests.

19. Changes in eating habits, indicating depression, emotional trauma, or lethargy.

20. Changes in sleeping habits; more time out late at night, on full moon nights and on satanic holy days.

21. Loss of interest in normal activities, replaced by time spent in secret or occult games.

22. Increased use of alcohol and/or drugs.

23. Sexual promiscuity; inappropriate sexual activities, tendencies and fantasies.

24. Intensified rebellion and rejection of Christian upbringing.

25. Cruelty to animals.

26. Cruelty to friends, family or other children.

27. Self-mutilation, such as cuts or cigarette burns, especially on the left arm.

28. Violent rage.

29. Getting involved in vandalism, especially of churches and cemeteries, and desecration of religious artifacts.

30. Hostility toward Christianity and Christ-centered topics, blessed objects, religious artifacts, prayer, the Bible, Christian symbols, church and spiritual discussions.

31. Obsessive thoughts of suicide, death, pain, rape, blood, torture or murder.

32. Objects used in rituals: eg., knives, chalices, bones (skulls and the short bones of hands and feet are favorites), gongs, drums, bells, candles, altar rock or slab or boards, ashes, graveyard dirt, robes with detachable

hoods, whips, small velvet pillow, empty cages, animal masks, black satin or velvet gloves, large ruby stone ring, incense, body or face paint, flash powder, coffin-like box.

All of these are signs that a person needs Christ's victory in their lives. The more signs that apply, the more deeply into Satan a person is. If you've noticed a trend toward increasingly greater involvement, or if there is evidence of actual devil worship, don't delay seeking help!

Symbols of Satanism and Black Witchcraft

PENTAGRAM

Five-pointed star within circle or double circle; with a goat's head inside the star, it's called "the Emblem of Baphomet".
Meaning: Two points up represent the devil's horns; three points down are a denial of the Holy Trinity; the goat is Satan, the rival of the Lamb, Jesus.

UPSIDE-DOWN CROSS
Meaning: Denial of Christianity; denial of Christ and His redemption through the cross.

PEACE SYMBOL or THE CROSS OF NERI

Upside-down cross with its arms broken, used by the Nazis, later used by the "free sex" and occult movement in the 1960s, as a symbol of "peace", ironically during an increase of the "battle" between morality and immorality.

Meaning: defeat Christ, Christianity and Christian morals.

SIGN OF CONFUSION
Meaning: Questions who really died on the cross, to throw in doubt that He was the Jesus that Christians teach (originated with the Romans in the first century A.D.)

EGYPTIAN ANKH CROSS
Meaning: Ancient Egyptians used this to symbolize *Ra*, the god of fertility and sex; Satan worshipers call it "the Cross of Satan" and believe it represents life, often using it in sex rituals.

SWASTIKA
Cross with each arm broken.
Meaning: Defeat Christ/Christianity; originated in ancient Mesopotamia as a symbol of good fortune, used by Eastern religions in connection with reincarnation, adopted by the Nazis through Guido von List who was involved in the occult, now used by satanists and witches during incantations.

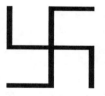

SEAL OF SOLOMON
Not to be confused with the five-pointed Jewish Star of David.
Meaning: The evil trinity (Satan, the Beast, the Anti-Christ) are merging with the fallen nature of man (pride, power, pleasure).

CRESCENT MOON & STAR(S)
Meaning: The moon represents the goddess Diana, the most important female deity of witchcraft; the stars represent Lucifer and his demons; together they represent Satan's claim that he is divine and sovereign.

SIGN OF THE BEAST
Three sixes or three Fs (the sixth letter).
Meaning: In the Book of *Revelations*, chapter 13, the Beast is one who resembles Christ but gives a demonic message and leads people to idolatry. Also note that the number 6 is one less than 7, the Biblical number for perfec-tion; 666 is triply less than perfect, or the height of imper-fection. Aleister Crowley, the founder of modern satanism, claimed to be mark-ed with this.

LIGHTNING BOLTS
Usually seen in pairs.
Meaning: Used by Hitler's secret society, which was occult-ic, now it's similarity to the letter "s" makes it an abbrevia-tion for Satan.

HORNED HAND
Not to be confused with the sign language symbol for "I love you," which includes the thumb held out.
Meaning: Satanic salute represent-ing the devil's horns.

ANARCHY
Meaning: Denial of authority; represents a desire for an all-out attack against Christians, the Pope and other moral authorities.

YIN-YANG
Meaning: Ancient eastern religious symbol originating in China and still used in the worship of gods; represents two complementary forces (male-female, earth-heaven, dark-light, good-evil; used in astrology and divination; popular with satanists because they believe evil is good and good is evil, pain is pleasure, death is life.

SWORD
Meaning: Used in satanic rituals as a tool for killing and torturing, it symbolizes aggressive force and power over the weak (note: satanists consider Christians weak).

NO CHRISTIANITY
Meaning: Christianity is a bad religion; say no to Christ and Christianity.

CHURCH OF SATAN
Meaning: Found in the *Satanic Bible*, it's a six-pointed cross (the two bottom loops are regarded as points) to represent Satan's reign as victorious over Christ and as everlasting.

SKULL AND CROSS BONES
Meaning: death.

MISCELLANEOUS

NATAS ("A"s may be triangles): Satan spelled backwards.

ZOSO: Three-headed dog, protector of gateway to hell; also the nickname of heavy metal singer Jimmy Page.

SWP: Supreme White Power (white supremacy term).

FTW: F — The World.

Appendix D

How to Intervene and Provide God's Help

Satanism is not a passing phase, and even milder forms of the occult lead to permanent bondage by demons unless Christ intervenes. It easily becomes an addiction. So how can we help? When is the right time to help?

Sometimes we hesitate because of fear, afraid that we might be reading too much into a person's behavior. We hope that things will change before we have to enforce change. However, occult addiction is at least as powerful as alcoholism or drugs. So it's safer to over-react than to under-react. Here are steps you can take to provide God's help to the person who needs it, especially to youth

1. Pray for the addict frequently, getting friends to add prayer support. Call upon God's power to weaken the demons in his (or her) life, through Jesus who already conquered Satan on the cross.

2. The question must be asked: "Why did this person become interested in this? What need is he trying to fill? What problems does he feel powerless to overcome?

3. Show genuine concern, not anger. Keep the lines of communication open. Discuss your worries in a loving and calm manner; don't sound judgmental, don't accuse. Find ways to affirm rather than always focusing on the bad behavior. Build up his self-esteem. Get in touch with his underlying emotional problems. Work to address those. And when you forbid certain activities (such as

playing with *Dungeons and Dragons* or going out on a satanic holy day), enforce it and be consistent. Use realistic punishment for disobedience, and reward obedience generously.

4. When he is ready to receive help, a combination of methods must be aggressively pursued. Find a Christian counselor who has a background in adolescent psychology, addiction recovery, and preferably the occult. Combine this with spiritual counseling that includes deliverance prayers for breaking the influence that the demons have had on him. Also, seek out a pastor or lay minister who is experienced in this. Even if the child or friend who needs the help refuses to go with you at first, go for yourself, so that you become better equipped to win the battle into which the Lord has placed you.

5. Family members must cooperate and make changes required of them, perhaps also receiving counseling and prayers. Parents should realize that they are not always to blame, but joining the child in the process of recovery gives him a sense of belonging to a caring family. Meanwhile, parents should learn all they can about the problem and find support from those who understand.

6. Jesus must be viewed as the greatest helper. Since those involved in the occult are seeking supernatural help, Christ must be shown as the better source of this help. His superior power must seem real, along with His unconditional love and generosity. "Why Jesus instead of occult powers?" The answer must become obvious. And the recovering addict must pursue Christian spiritual growth at least as actively as he had pursued satanic spiritual growth, in order to resist the pull back to occult interests that will repeatedly occur.

Appendix E

What Does God Say About the Occult?

(Over 180 Scripture References)
Note: Since this entire Appendix is composed of direct
Scriptural passages, italics for the passages is eliminated.

CONTENTS

1. Do All Supernatural Powers Come From God?

The Bible clearly says that some supernatural gifts come from God and some do not. There are those that come to us from God the Father, through Jesus Christ. And there are those that come to us from Satan the father of lies, through his demons. What Jesus offers is, of course, by far the best.

The Bible often refers to Jesus as "Light" and the dominion of Satan as "Darkness." The word "occult," as a verb, means "to deliberately hide from sight, to keep secret, to conceal or extinguish the light of by intervention" (*Webster's New International Dictionary*). Demons, through the occult, try to hide or extinguish the Light of Christ.

Key verse: John 14:12 (TLB) — Anyone believing in me [Jesus] shall do the same miracles I have done, and even greater ones, because I am going to be with the Father.

Luke 1:79 (NJB) — [Jesus came] to give light to those who live/ in darkness . . . to guide our feet/ into the way of peace.

John 3:19, 20 (NIV) — Light has come into the world, but men loved darkness instead of light because their deeds were evil. Everyone who does evil hates the light, and will not come into the light for fear that his deeds will be exposed.

John 8:12 (NIV) — I am the light of the world. Whoever follows me will never walk in darkness, but will have the light of life.

John 12:46 (TLB) — I have come as a Light to shine in this dark world, so that all who put their trust in me will no longer wander in the darkness.

John 14:6 (NIV) — I am the way and the truth and the life. No one comes to the Father except through me.

Rom. 13:12 (NIV) — Let us put aside the deeds of darkness and put on the armor of light.

Eph. 5:8-11 (TLB) — Though once your heart was full of darkness, now it is full of light from the Lord, and your behavior should show it! Because of this light within you, you should do only what is good and right and true. Learn as you go along what pleases the Lord. Take no part in the worthless pleasures of evil and darkness, but instead, rebuke and expose them.

1 John 1:5, 6 (NIV) — God is light; in him there is no darkness at all. If we claim to have fellowship with him yet walk in the darkness, we lie and do not live by the truth.

2. The Deceivers: Satan and His Demons

Key verse: 1 Cor. 10:20, 21 (NIV) — The sacrifices of pagans are offered to demons, not to God, and I do not want you to be participants with demons. You cannot drink the cup of the Lord and the cup of demons too; you cannot have a part in both the Lord's table and the table of demons.

Satan's Origins

Is. 14:12-15 (TLB) — How you are fallen from heaven, O Lucifer, son of the morning! . . . For you said to yourself, "I will ascend to heaven and rule the angels. I will take the highest throne. I will . . . be like the Most High." But instead, you will be brought down to the pit of hell.

Ezek. 28:12, 15-17 (RSV) — You [Satan] were the signet of perfection,/ full of wisdom/ and perfect in beauty./ . . . You were blameless in your ways/ from the day you were created,/ till iniquity was found in you./ In the abundance of your trade/ you were filled with violence, and you sinned;/ so I cast you as a profane thing from the mountain of God/ . . . Your heart was proud because of your beauty;/ you corrupted your wisdom for the sake of your splendor.

2 Pet. 2:4 (RSV) — God did not spare the angels when they sinned, but cast them down into hell and committed them to pits of nether gloom to be kept until the judgment.

Jude 6 (NIV) — The angels who did not keep their positions of authority but abandoned their own home — these he has kept in darkness, bound with everlasting chains for judgment on the great Day.

Rev. 12:4 (NIV) — His tail swept a third of the stars out of the sky and flung them to the earth. [Satan took a third of the angels with him in the fall from Heaven.]

Rev. 12:7-9 (NIV) — And there was war in heaven. Michael and his angels fought against the dragon, and the dragon and his angels fought back. But he was not strong enough, and they lost their place in heaven. The great dragon was hurled down — that ancient serpent called the devil or Satan, who leads the whole world astray. He was hurled to the earth, and his angels with him.

Satan's Nature

John 8:44 (RSV) — [Satan] has nothing to do with the truth, because there is no truth in him. When he lies, he speaks according to his own nature, for he is a liar and the father of lies.

James 2:19 (GNB) — Do you believe that there is only one God? Good! The demons also believe — and tremble with fear.

1 John 2:22, 23 (NIV) — Who is the liar? It is the man who denies that Jesus is the Christ. Such a man is the antichrist — he denies the Father and the Son. No one who denies the Son has the Father.

Satan's Activities

Job 1:7 (NJB) — Yahweh said to Satan, "Where have you

been?" "Prowling about on the earth," he answered, "roaming around there."

Matt. 4:8-11 (RSV) — The devil . . . showed him all the kingdoms of the world and the glory of them; and he said to him, "All these I will give you, if you will fall down and worship me." Then Jesus said to him, "Begone, Satan! for it is written, "You shall worship the Lord your God and him only shall you serve."

Matt. 12:30 (NIV) — He who is not with me [Jesus] is against me, and he who does not gather with me scatters.

John 10:1, 10 (RSV) — He who does not enter the sheepfold by the door [through Jesus] but climbs in by another way, that man is a thief and a robber . . . The thief [Satan or some other deceiving demon] comes only to steal and kill and destroy.

1 Cor. 7:5 (NJB) — Satan may take advantage of any lack of self-control to put you to the test.

2 Thess. 2:9, 10 (GNB) — The Wicked One will come with the power of Satan and perform all kinds of miracles and false signs and wonders, and use every kind of wicked deceit.

1 Pet. 5:8, 9 (NIV) — Be self-controlled and alert. Your enemy the devil prowls around like a roaring lion looking for someone to devour. Resist him, standing firm in the faith.

2 John 7 (NIV) — Many deceivers, who do not acknowledge Jesus Christ . . . have gone out into the world. Any such person is the deceiver and the antichrist.

Rev. 16:13, 14 (TLB) — I saw three evil spirits disguised as frogs leap from the mouth of the Dragon, the Creature, and his False Prophet. These miracle-working demons conferred with all the rulers of the world to gather them for battle against the Lord.

Demon Powers

Matt. 8:28, 29 (NIV) — Two demon-possessed men coming from the tombs met him. They were so violent that no one could pass that way. "What do you want with us, Son of God?" they shouted. "Have you come here to torture us before the appointed time?" [Demons recognize Jesus' divinity and know their future fate —see also Mark 1:23, 24.]

Matt. 12:43-45 (NIV) — When an evil spirit comes out of a man, it goes . . . seeking rest and does not find it. Then it says, "I will return to the home I left." [Demons prefer to possess someone rather than roam loose.] When it arrives, it finds the house unoccupied [the person needs Jesus to fill the void] . . . Then it goes and takes with it seven other spirits more wicked than itself, and they go in and live there. And the final condition of that man is worse than the first. [See also Luke 11:24-26.]

Mark 5:3, 4 (TLB) — [A demon-possessed man] lived among the gravestones, and had such strength that whenever he was put into handcuffs and shackles —as he often was —he snapped the handcuffs from his wrists and smashed the shackles and walked away. No one was strong enough to control him. [Demons give people supernormal strength.]

Mark 5:9, 10, 12 (NIV) — Then Jesus asked him [the demon], "What is your name?" "My name is Legion," he replied, "for we are many." [A person can be in bondage to many demons.] And he begged Jesus again and again not to send them out of the area. [Demons fear being sent away.] . . . "Send us among the pigs, allow us to go into them." [Demons can possess animals.]

Satan Is Conquered

Matt. 25:40, 41 (TLB) — I, the King [Jesus], will tell them [the wicked], . . . "Away with you, you cursed ones, into the eternal fire prepared for the devil and his demons."

John 16:11 (NJB) — The prince of this world is already condemned.

2 Thess. 2:8 (GNB) — The Wicked One will appear, and the Lord Jesus will . . . destroy him with his glorious appearing, when he comes.

Rev. 12:10, 11 (RSV) — [Satan] the accuser of our brethren has been thrown down, who accuses them day and night before our God [trying to get us in trouble]. And they have conquered him by the blood of the Lamb and by the word of their testimony.

3. Deceptions of the Occult

Key verse: 2 Cor. 6:16 (NJB) — The temple of God cannot compromise with false gods, and that is what we are — the temple of the living God.

Demons Are Behind the Occult

Deut. 32:17 (RSV) — They sacrificed to demons which were no gods [as a result of pagan influence].

Matt. 7:15 (RSV) — Beware of false prophets, who come to you in sheep's clothing but inwardly are ravenous wolves.

2 Cor. 4:4 (RSV) — The god of this world [Satan] has blinded the minds of the unbelievers, to keep them from seeing the light of the gospel.

2 Cor. 11:14 (RSV) — Satan disguises himself as an angel of light. So it is not strange if his servants also disguise themselves as servants of righteousness.

Gal. 4:8, 9 (RSV) — When you did not know God, you were in bondage to beings that by nature are no gods; but now that you have come to know God . . . how can you turn back again to the weak and beggarly elemental spirits, whose slaves you want to be once more? [A good argument against celebrating Halloween!]

Col. 2:8 (NIV) — See to it that no one takes you captive through hollow and deceptive philosophy, which depends on human tradition and the basic principles of this world rather than on Christ.

1 Tim. 4:1 (RSV) — The Spirit expressly says that in later times some will depart from the faith by giving heed to deceitful spirits and doctrines of demons.

1 John 3:7 (NIV) — Do not let anyone lead you astray.

The Results of Deception

Is. 5:20 (NIV) — Woe to those who call evil good/ and good evil,/ who put darkness for light/ and light for darkness.

Is. 26:18 (NJB) — We have been pregnant [with ideas, power, spirituality, etc.] . . . but we have given birth only to wind:/ we have not given salvation to the earth.

Matt. 13:19 (NIV) — When anyone hears the message about the kingdom and does not understand it, the evil one comes and snatches away what was sown in his heart.

Rom. 1:21 (TLB) — They knew about him [God] all right, but . . . after awhile they began to think up silly ideas of what God was like and what he wanted them to do. The result was that their foolish minds became dark and confused.

Rom. 1:22, 23, 25 (NJB) — While they claimed to be wise, in fact they were growing so stupid that they exchanged the glory of the immortal God for an imitation . . . they exchanged God's truth for a lie.

2 Tim. 3:2-7 (RSV) — Men will be lovers of self . . . unholy, inhuman . . . treacherous, reckless . . . lovers of pleasure rather than lovers of God, holding the form of religion but denying the power of it. Avoid such people. For among them are those . . . who will listen to anybody and can

never arrive at a knowledge of the truth.

2 Pet. 2:1-3 (NIV) — There will be false teachers among you. They will secretly introduce destructive heresies, even denying the sovereign Lord who bought them — bringing swift destruction on themselves. Many will follow their shameful ways and will bring the way of truth into disrepute. In their greed these teachers will exploit you.

1 John 1:6 (NIV) — If we claim to have fellowship with him [God] yet walk in the darkness, we lie and do not live by the truth.

False Christs

Mark 13:21, 22 (NIV) — If anyone says to you, "Look, here is the Christ!" or, "Look, there he is!" do not believe it. For false Christs and false prophets will appear and perform signs and miracles to deceive the elect. [See also Matthew 24:23, 24.]

Luke 17:1, 2 (NIV) — Things that cause people to sin are bound to come, but woe to that person through whom they come. It would be better for him to be thrown into the sea with a millstone tied around his neck. [See also Matthew 18:6,7 and Mark 9:42.]

Luke 21:8 (GNB) — Jesus said, "Watch out; don't be fooled. Because many men will come in my name saying, "I am he!" . . . But don't follow them."

2 Cor. 11:3, 4 (GNB) — I am afraid that your minds will be corrupted and that you will abandon your full and pure devotion to Christ — in the same way that Eve was deceived by the snake's clever lies. For you gladly tolerate anyone who comes to you and preaches a different Jesus . . . and you accept a spirit and a gospel completely different from the Spirit and the gospel you received from us!

4. Psychic Powers

In biblical times, as today, magic was performed to influence people and events by supernatural means, usually with the aid of a spirit. Divination was often a part of the practice of magic and was a general term describing all attempts to obtain information from the spiritual world without going to God.

Key verse: Deut. 18:10-12 (NJB) — There must never be anyone . . . who practises divination, who is soothsayer, augur or sorcerer, weaver of spells, consulter of ghosts or mediums, or necromancer. For anyone who does these things is detestable to Yahweh.

2 Kings 21:6 (TLB) — He practiced black magic and used fortune-telling, and patronized mediums and wizards. So the Lord was very angry, for Manasseh was an evil man, in God's sight. [Also in 2 Chronicles 33:6.]

Jer. 27:9, 10 (NIV) — Do not listen to your prophets, your diviners, your interpreters of dreams, your mediums or your sorcerers [those who contradict God's Word] . . . They prophesy lies to you . . . and you will perish.

2 Tim. 2:12 (GNB) — If we deny him [Christ Jesus],/ he also will deny us.

Heb. 10:29 (NJB) — Anyone who tramples on the Son of God, and who treats the blood of the covenant which sanctified him as if it were not holy . . . will be condemned to a far severer punishment.

Fortune Telling, Ouija Boards, Divination

Deut. 18:14, 15 (RSV) — These nations . . . give heed to soothsayers and diviners; but as for you, the Lord your God has not allowed you so to do. The Lord your God will raise up for you a prophet [Jesus] . . . him you shall heed.

Deut. 18:20 (NIV) — A prophet who presumes to speak in

my name anything I have not commanded him to say, or a prophet who speaks in the name of other gods, must be put to death.

2 Kings 17:16, 17 (RSV) — They forsook all the commandments of the Lord . . . and used divination and sorcery, and sold themselves to do evil in the sight of the Lord, provoking him to anger.

Is. 44:25 (NJB) — I [Yahweh] . . . foil the omens of soothsayers/ and make fools of diviners.

Jer. 14:14 (NIV) — The prophets are prophesying lies in my name. I have not sent them or appointed them or spoken to them. They are prophesying to you false visions, divinations, idolatries and the delusions of their own minds.

Ezek. 13:7, 8 (RSV) — "Have you not seen a delusive vision, and uttered a lying divination, whenever you have said, "Says the Lord," although I have not spoken?" Therefore thus says the Lord God: ". . . I am against you."

Ezek. 13:23 (NAB) — You shall no longer see false visions and practice divination, but I will rescue my people from your power.

Ezek. 22:28 (TLB) — Your "prophets" describe false visions and speak false messages they claim are from God, when he hasn't spoken one word to them at all.

Hos. 4:12 (RSV) — My people inquire of a thing of wood [used for divination],/ and their staff gives them oracles./ For a spirit of harlotry has led them astray,/ and they have left their God to play the harlot.

Mic. 3:11 (RSV) — [Unfaithful] prophets divine for money; / yet they lean upon the Lord and say,/ "Is not the Lord in the midst of us?/ No evil shall come upon us." [But because divination is sin, disaster will strike —verse 12].

Zech. 10:2 (NIV) — Diviners see visions that lie;/ they tell dreams that are false,/ they give comfort in vain./ Therefore the people wander like sheep,/ oppressed for lack of a shepherd. [Jesus is the Shepherd we need.]

Matt. 7:21-23 (NIV) — Not everyone who says to me, "Lord, Lord," will enter the kingdom of heaven, but only he who does the will of my Father who is in heaven. Many will say to me on that day, "Lord, Lord, did we not prophesy in your name, and in your name drive out demons and perform many miracles?" Then I will tell them plainly, "I never knew you. Away from me, you evildoers!" [This applies to psychics who claim a partnership with God.]

Acts 16:16-18 (NIV) — We were met by a slave girl who had a spirit by which she predicted the future. She earned a great deal of money for her owners by fortune-telling . . . Finally Paul . . . said to the spirit, "In the name of Jesus Christ I command you to come out of her!" At that moment the spirit left her.

Astrology

The Hebrews believed that spirit beings, called "the host or army of heaven," controlled the movements of stars and planets.

Deut. 4:19 (NJB) — The sun, the moon, the stars . . . do not be tempted to worship them and serve them.

Deut. 17:2-5 (NJB) — If there is anyone . . . who goes and serves . . . the sun or the moon or any of heaven's array — a thing I have forbidden —. . . you must stone that man or woman to death.

2 Kings 17:16, 17 (TLB) — They defied all the commandments of the Lord . . . They made detestable, shameful idols and worshiped . . . the sun, moon, and stars . . . . They consulted fortune-tellers and used magic and sold themselves to evil. So the Lord was very angry.

2 Kings 21:2, 3 (NJB) — [King Manasseh] did what is displeasing to Yahweh . . . he worshipped the whole array of heaven and served it. [Repeated in 2 Chronicles 33:2, 3.]

Is. 47:13, 14 (TLB) — You have advisors by the ton —your astrologers and stargazers, who try to tell you what the future holds. But they are as useless as dried grass burning in the fire. They cannot even deliver themselves! You'll get no help from them at all.

Jer. 10:2 (NIV) — Do not learn the ways of the nations/ or be terrified by signs in the sky.

Acts 7:42 (NIV) — God turned away and gave them over to the worship of the heavenly bodies.

Mediums, Channeling, Spirits

Lev. 19:31 (NIV) — Do not turn to mediums or seek out spiritists, for you will be defiled by them.

Lev. 20:6 (NIV) — I will set my face against the person who turns to mediums and spiritists.

1 Sam. 28 — [King Saul seeks help from a medium after refusing to listen to prophets and dreams through which God warned him to repent. He asks her to conjure up the prophet Samuel. She sees a ghost, which Saul assumes to be Samuel. Because of his sin, Saul is soon killed in battle. See 1 Chron. 10:13, 14.]

2 Kings 23:24 (TLB) — Josiah [King of Judah] also exterminated the mediums and wizards . . . For Josiah wanted to follow all the laws.

1 Chron. 10:13, 14 (NIV) — Saul died because he was unfaithful to the Lord; he . . . consulted a medium for guidance, and did not inquire of the Lord.

Is. 8:19 (TLB) — So why are you trying to find out the future by consulting witches and mediums? Don't listen to their whisperings and mutterings. Can the living find out the future from the dead? Why not ask your God?

Is. 28:15, 16 (NAB) — Because you say, "We have made a covenant with death,/ and with the nether world . . . we have made lies our refuge,/ and in falsehood we have found a hiding place," —/ Therefore, thus says the Lord God:/ See, I am laying a stone in Zion [Jesus Christ] . . . he who puts his faith in it shall not be shaken.

1 Tim. 2:5, 6 (NJB) — For there is only one God, and there is only one mediator between God and humanity . . . Christ Jesus, who offered himself as a ransom for all.

1 Pet. 3:19, 20 (RSV) — [In spirit, Jesus] went and preached to the spirits [of the dead] in prison, who formerly did not obey. [Since they are imprisoned, they cannot speak to us!]

Reincarnation

Although there are only a few scriptures directly pertaining to reincarnation, the whole Gospel message proves that multiple lives are impossible.

Is. 26:14 (NJB) — The dead [those who die without Christ] will not come back to life . . . for you [Yahweh] have punished them.

1 Cor. 15:21, 22 (GNB) — Just as death came by means of a man [Adam], in the same way the rising from death comes by means of a man [Jesus]. For just as all men die because of their union to Adam, in the same way all will be raised to life because of their union to Christ.

2 Cor. 5:1 (TLB) — When this tent we live in now is taken down —when we die and leave these bodies —we will have wonderful new bodies in heaven, homes that will be ours forever more, made for us by God himself, and not by human hands.

Gal. 5:1 (NJB) — Christ set us free, so that we should remain free. Stand firm, then, and do not let yourselves be fastened again to the yoke of slavery.

Col. 2:14, 15 (GNB) — [Jesus] canceled the unfavorable record of our debts, with its binding rules [e.g., Karma], and did away with it completely by nailing it to the cross.

Heb. 9:27 (RSV) — It is appointed for men to die once, and after that comes judgement.

Sorcery and Witchcraft

Gen. 41 — [Joseph, with God's help, interprets the pharaoh's dream after all the magicians and wise men of Egypt have failed.]

Ex. 7:10-12 (TLB) — Moses and Aaron went in to see Pharaoh, and performed the miracle, as Jehovah had instructed them — Aaron threw down his rod before Pharaoh and his court, and it became a serpent. Then the Pharaoh called in his sorcerers — the magicians of Egypt — and they were able to do the same thing with their magical arts! But Aaron's serpent swallowed their serpents [proving God's superiority]!

Ex. 20:3 (NJB) — You shall have no other gods to rival me [no source of supernatural power or knowledge except God].

Ex. 22:18 (RSV) — You shall not permit a sorceress to live.

Lev. 19:26 (NIV) — Do not practice divination or sorcery.

Num. 23:23 (NIV) — There is no sorcery against Jacob, no divination against Israel [a curse simply would not work against God's people].

1 Sam. 15:23 (NJB) — Rebellion is a sin of sorcery.

Is. 1:13, 14 (NJB) — New Moons, Sabbaths, assemblies — I cannot endure solemnity combined with guilt./ Your New Moons and your meetings I utterly detest.

Is. 2:6 (TLB) — The Lord has rejected you because you welcome foreigners . . . who practice magic and communicate with evil spirits.

Is. 3:18-21 (NJB) — The Lord will take away the ornamental chains, medallions, crescents, pendants . . . amulets . . . [He doesn't want us to use charms or wear occult symbols.]

Is. 47:9, 11 (NJB) — Bereavement . . ./ will suddenly befall you/ in spite of all your witchcraft/ and the potency of your spells./ . . . Disaster will befall you/ which you will not know how to charm away.

Is. 57:3, 4 (NAB) — You sons of a sorceress,/ adulterous, wanton race!/ . . . Are you not rebellious children?

Dan. 1:20 (RSV) — In every matter of wisdom and understanding which the king inquired of [Daniel, Hananiah, Mishael and Azariah], he found them ten times better than all the magicians and enchanters.

Dan. 2:27, 28 (NIV) — No wise man, enchanter, magician or diviner can explain to the king the mystery . . . but there is a God in heaven who reveals mysteries.

Dan. 4 and 5 — [The wise men, enchanters, magicians and diviners fail to interpret another of King Nebuchadnezzar's dreams, and Daniel succeeds with God's help.] [Soothsayers fail to interpret handwriting on the wall at Crown Prince Belshazzar's banquet, but Daniel succeeds.]

Mic. 5:12 (NIV) — I will destroy your witchcraft/ and you will no longer cast spells.

Nah. 3:4-5 (TLB) — The beautiful and faithless city, mistress of deadly charms, enticed the nations . . . then taught them all to worship her false gods, bewitching people everywhere. "No wonder I stand against you," says the Lord Almighty.

Mal. 3:5 (RSV) — I will be a swift witness against the

sorcerers.

Acts 13:6, 9-11 (RSV) — They came upon a certain magician, a Jewish false prophet, named Bar-Jesus . . . . Paul, filled with the Holy Spirit, looked intently at him and said, "You son of the devil, you enemy of all righteousness, full of all deceit and villainy, will you not stop making crooked the straight paths of the Lord? And now, behold, the hand of the Lord is upon you, and you shall be blind and unable to see the sun for a time." Immediately mist and darkness fell upon him.

Acts 19:18, 19 (NIV) — Many of those who believed now came and openly confessed their evil deeds. A number who had practiced sorcery brought their scrolls together and burned them publicly.

Gal. 5:19-21 (NIV) — The acts of the sinful nature are obvious: . . . idolatry and witchcraft . . . and the like. I warn you . . . those who live like this will not inherit the kingdom of God.

Rev. 21:8 (TLB) — Cowards who turn back from following me, and those who are unfaithful to me . . . and those conversing with demons . . . and all liars — their doom is in the Lake that burns with fire and sulphur. This is the Second Death.

Rev. 22:15 (RSV) — Outside [of heavenly Jerusalem] are the dogs and sorcerers . . . and everyone who loves and practices falsehood.

5. Testing the Source of Supernatural Power

Key verse: 1 Thess. 5:20-23 (TLB) — Do not scoff at those who prophesy, but test everything that is said to be sure it is true, and if it is, then accept it. Keep away from every kind of evil. May the God of peace himself make you entirely pure and devoted to God.

Whom Does It Serve?

Deut. 13:1-3, 5 (RSV) — If a prophet arises among you . . . and gives you a sign or wonder, and the sign or wonder which he tells you comes to pass, and if he says, "Let us go after other gods . . . and let us serve them," you shall not listen to the words of that prophet . . . That prophet . . . has taught rebellion against the Lord your God.

Rom. 8:14 (NIV) — Those who are led by the Spirit of God are sons of God.

1 John 3:8 (NIV) — He who does what is sinful is of the devil, because the devil has been sinning from the beginning.

Does It Acknowledge Jesus Christ?

John 15:23 (NIV) — He who hates me [Jesus] hates my Father as well.

1 John 4:1-3 (TLB) — Don't always believe everything you hear just because someone says it is a message from God: test it first to see if it really is. For there are many false teachers around, and the way to find out if their message is from the Holy Spirit is to ask: Does it really agree that Jesus Christ, God's Son, actually became man with a human body? If so, then the message is from God. If not, the message is not from God but from one who is against Christ, like the "Antichrist."

1 John 4:15 (NIV) — If anyone acknowledges that Jesus is the Son of God, God lives in him and he in God.

Does It Agree With God's Word?

Is. 8:20 (TLB) — "Check these witches' words against the Word of God!" he says. "If their messages are different than mine, it is because I have not sent them; for they have no light or truth in them.

Heb. 4:12, 13 (GNB) — The word of God is alive and active. It is sharper than any double-edged sword. It cuts all the way through, to where soul and spirit meet . . . It judges the desires and thoughts of men's hearts . . . . Everything in all creation is exposed.

2 John 9-11 (TLB) — If you wander beyond the teaching of Christ, you will leave God behind; while if you are loyal to Christ's teachings, you will have God too . . . . If anyone comes to teach you, and he doesn't believe what Christ taught, don't even invite him into your home. Don't encourage him in any way. If you do you will be a partner with him in his wickedness.

What Are Its Fruits?

Prov. 10:9 (NJB) — Anyone whose ways are honourable walks secure,/ but whoever follows crooked ways is soon unmasked.

Matt. 7:16, 17 (NJB) — You will be able to tell them by their fruits . . . . A sound tree produces good fruit but a rotten tree bad fruit.

Rom. 14:17 (NIV) — The kingdom of God is . . . righteousness, peace and joy in the Holy Spirit.

Gal. 5:19-23 (NIV) — The acts of the sinful nature are obvious: sexual immorality . . . idolatry and witchcraft . . . and the like. I warn you, as I did before, that those who live like this will not inherit the kingdom of God. But the fruit of the Spirit is love, joy, peace, patience, kindness, goodness, faithfulness, gentleness and self-control.

God Gives Us Discernment

Rom. 12:2 (GNB) — Do not conform outwardly to the standards of this world, but let God transform you inwardly by a complete change of your mind. Then you will be able to know the will of God.

1 John 5:20 (NIV) — The Son of God has come and has given us understanding, so that we may know him who is true.

6. Spiritual Warfare

Spiritual warfare helps us live victoriously. It also enables us to help others who are living in darkness. The world is a battlefield between Christ and Satan. If we put on the armor of God and fight, we will not become victims of the war, but conquerors.

Key verse: Eph. 6:10-12 (NIV) — Be strong in the Lord and in his mighty power. Put on the full armor of God so that you can take your stand against the devil's schemes. For our struggle is not against flesh and blood, but against the rulers, against the authorities, against the powers of this dark world and against the spiritual forces of evil in the heavenly realms.

God Rescues Us

Psalm 91:3, 4 (NJB) — He rescues you from the snare/ of the fowler set on destruction/. . . His constancy is shield and protection.

Matt. 6:9, 10, 13 (TLB) — Pray along these lines: "Our Father in heaven, we honor your holy name. We ask that your kingdom will come now. May your will be done here on earth, just as it is in heaven . . . . deliver us from the Evil One.

Luke 4:18 (GNB) — He has sent me [Jesus] to proclaim liberty to the captives/ . . . to set free the oppressed.

Acts 10:38 (NJB) — Jesus went about doing good and curing all who had fallen into the power of the devil.

Acts 26:17, 18 (GNB) — I will save you from the people . . . to whom I will send you. You are to open their eyes and turn them from the darkness to the light, and from the power of Satan to God.

Rom. 16:20 (NIV) — The God of peace will soon crush Satan under your feet.

1 Cor. 10:13 (NAB) — God keeps his promise. He will not let you be tested beyond your strength. Along with the test he will give you a way out of it so that you may be able to endure it.

Eph. 3:20 (TLB) — Now glory be to God who by his mighty power at work within us is able to do far more than we would ever dare to ask or even dream of — infinitely beyond our highest prayers, desires, thoughts, or hopes.

Col. 1:13 (TLB) — For [God] has rescued us out of the darkness and gloom of Satan's kingdom and brought us into the Kingdom of his dear Son.

2 Thess. 3:3 (NJB) — You can rely on the Lord, who will give you strength and guard you from the evil One.

2 Tim. 1:7 (KJV) — God hath not given us the spirit of fear; but of power, and of love, and of a sound mind.

The Victory of Jesus

John 12:31, 32 (NAB) — Now has judgment come upon this world,/ now will this world's prince be driven out,/ and I — once I am lifted up from the earth —/ will draw all men to myself.

John 14:30 (TLB) — The evil prince of this world approaches. He has no power over me.

John 16:33 (NJB) — Find peace in me / . . . Be courageous:/ I have conquered the world.

Rom. 8:37-39 (NIV) — In all these things we are more than conquerors through him who loved us. For I am convinced that neither death nor life, neither angels nor demons, neither the present nor the future, nor any powers, neither height nor depth, nor anything else in all creation, will be able to separate us from the love of God that is in Christ Jesus our Lord.

1 Cor. 15:24, 25 (NIV) — Then the end will come, when he hands over the kingdom to God the Father after he has destroyed all dominion, authority and power. For he must reign until he has put all his enemies under his feet.

Gal. 1:4 (NIV) — [Jesus] gave himself for our sins to rescue us from the present evil age.

Gal. 5:1 (NIV) — It is for freedom that Christ has set us free. Stand firm, then, and do not let yourselves be burdened again by a yoke of slavery.

Eph. 1:19, 21 (GNB) — How very great is his power at work in us who believe. . . . Christ rules . . . above all heavenly rulers, authorities, powers, and lords.

Phil. 2:9, 10 (GNB) — God raised him to the highest place above,/ and gave him the name that is greater than any other name./ And so, in honor of the name of Jesus,/ all beings in heaven, on earth, and in the world below/ will fall on their knees.

Col. 2:15 (NIV) — Having disarmed the powers and authorities, [Jesus] made a public spectacle of them, triumphing over them by the cross.

Heb. 2:14, 15 (NAB) — Since the children are men of blood and flesh, Jesus likewise had a full share in ours, that by his death he might rob the devil, the prince of death, of his power, and free those who . . . had been slaves.

1 John 3:8 (NIV) — The reason the Son of God appeared was to destroy the devil's work.

Angels Help Us

Psalm 34:7 (TLB) — The Angel of the Lord guards and

rescues all who reverence him.

Psalm 91:10-12 (NAB) — No evil shall befall you/ . . . For to his angels he has given command about you,/ that they guard you in all your ways./ Upon their hands they shall bear you up.

Heb. 1:14 (TLB) — The angels are only spirit-messengers sent out to help and care for those who are to receive his salvation.

The Authority of Believers

Mark 6:7 (NIV) — He sent them out two by two and gave them authority over evil spirits. [See also Matthew 10:1; Mark 3:14, 15; and Luke 9:1.]

Mark 16:17 (NIV) — These signs will accompany those who believe: In my name they will drive out demons . . .

Luke 10:17-19 (TLB) — When the seventy disciples return-ed, they joyfully reported to him, "Even the demons obey us when we use your name." "Yes," he told them, "I saw Satan falling from heaven as a flash of lightning! And I have given you authority over all the power of the Enemy . . Nothing shall injure you!"

Acts 1:8 (NJB) — You will receive the power of the Holy Spirit.

1 Cor. 3:16 (NIV) — Don't you know that you yourselves are God's temple and that God's Spirit lives in you? [See also 1 Cor. 6:19.]

2 Cor. 10:4 (NIV) — The weapons we fight with are not the weapons of the world. On the contrary, they have divine power to demolish strongholds.

Phil. 4:13 (TLB) — I can do everything God asks me to with the help of Christ who gives me strength and power.

2 Pet. 1:3, 4 (NIV) — His divine power has given us

everything we need . . . He has given us his very great and precious promises, so that through them you may participate in the divine nature.

1 John 4:4 (RSV) — You are of God, and have overcome them [evil spirits]; for he who is in you is greater than he who is in the world.

Rev. 12:11 (RSV) — They have conquered [Satan] by the blood of the Lamb and by the word of their testimony.

Binding and Casting Out

Matt. 12:29 (TLB) — One cannot rob Satan's kingdom without first binding Satan. Only then can his demons be cast out!

Matt. 16:19 (NIV) — Whatever you bind on earth will be bound in heaven, and whatever you loose on earth will be loosed in heaven. [See also Matthew 18:18.]

Col. 3:17 (NJB) — Whatever you say or do, let it be in the name of the Lord Jesus.

Truth as a Weapon

Psalm 119:104, 105 (NAB) — Through your precepts I gain discernment;/ therefore I hate every false way./ A lamp to my feet is your word,/ a light to my path.

Hos. 4:6 (NIV) — My people are destroyed from lack of knowledge.

John 8:31, 32 (NAB) — Jesus then went on to say . . .: "If you live according to my teaching,/ you are truly my disciples;/ then you will know the truth,/ and the truth will set you free."

John 14:26 (NIV) — The Counselor, the Holy Spirit, whom the Father will send in my name, will teach you all things.

John 16:13 (NJB) — When the Spirit of truth comes/ he

will lead you to the complete truth.

Acts 8:11-13 (NAB) — Those who followed [Simon, a Samaritan psychic] had been under the spell of his magic over a long period; but once they began to believe in the good news that Philip preached about the kingdom of God and the name of Jesus Christ, men and women alike accepted baptism. Even Simon believed.

2 Tim. 2:24-26 (NAB) — He [the servant of the Lord] must be an apt teacher, patiently and gently correcting those who contradict him, in the hope always that God will enable them to repent and know the truth. Thus, taken captive by God to do his will, they shall escape the devil's trap.

2 Tim. 3:16, 17 (NJB) — All scripture is inspired by God and useful for refuting error, for guiding people's lives and teaching them to be upright. This is how someone . . . becomes fully equipped.

Faith as a Weapon

Mark 9:23, 24 (RSV) — Jesus said . . . "All things are possible to him who believes." Immediately the father of the [demon-possessed] child cried out and said, "I believe; help my unbelief!"

Luke 22:31, 32 (GNB) — Satan has received permission to test all of you, as a farmer separates the wheat from the chaff. But I have prayed for you . . . that your faith will not fail. And when you turn back to me, you must strengthen your brothers.

1 Tim. 1:18, 19 (NJB) — Fight like a good soldier with faith and a good conscience for your weapons.

Heb. 12:2 (NAB) — Let us keep our eyes fixed on Jesus, who inspires and perfects our faith.

242

The Protection of Christian Living

Acts 19:13, 15, 16 (RSV) — Jewish exorcists undertook to pronounce the name of the Lord Jesus over those who had evil spirits . . . But the evil spirit answered them, "Jesus I know, and Paul I know; but who are you?" And the man in whom the evil spirit was leaped on them . . . and overpowered them. [Being a disciple of Jesus is necessary.]

2 Cor. 6:6, 7 (GNB) — By our purity, knowledge, patience, and kindness we have shown ourselves to be God's servants; by the Holy Spirit, by our true love, by our message of truth, and by the power of God. We have righteousness as our weapon, both to attack and to defend ourselves.

Eph. 5:11, 15-17 (NIV) — Have nothing to do with the fruitless deeds of darkness, but rather expose them. . . . Be very careful, then, how you live —not as unwise but as wise, making the most of every opportunity, because the days are evil. Therefore do not be foolish, but understand what the Lord's will is.

James 4:7 (NIV) — Submit yourselves, then, to God. Resist the devil, and he will flee from you.

THE END